<u>Dating Success</u>
AFTER 40

Dear Dad —
you are my hero
and role — model. This
is the 1st book printed
and I want you to have
it.   with love —
                    Mike
                    2·15·2014

Dating Success
AFTER 40

Nancy Michaels & Neil Wood

Table Of Contents

Nancy Michaels & Neil Wood

Acknowledgements

We are so indebted to our mutual friend, Mark Magnacca, for bringing the two of us together and ultimately, to collaborate on this project. Without him, we would not have met and had such a fun time writing this book for our fellow single friends, ages 40 and up. Thanks so much Mark!

Given that this is a book on dating, we need to thank our past "matches" and relationships who have helped us learn more about ourselves, what we want, and what we are seeking in our current (Neil) and future (Nancy) partners. Steve Harvey, if you're out there, Nancy would like a fix up!

We have immense gratitude to our panel of experts we interviewed. They provided exceptional breadth and depth to the book that would not have been possible without them. They include Stacey Alcorn, Anthony Ambrose, Cija Black, Ginger Burr, Dr. Diana Kirschner, Ande Lyons, Susan Ortolano, Rosalind Sedacca, Kimberly Seltzer, Robert Siciliano, Jodi R. R. Smith, Emmi Sorokin, Roseanne Thomas, Robyn Vogel and Susan Winter.

Oftentimes some of the most challenging circumstances in our lives become our greatest gifts and growth experiences. Our past marriages have blessed us with six children between us and we have overwhelming and unconditional love for them. Thank you Nick, Tim, Audrey, Chloe, Noah and Sophie.

Huge thanks go to our amazing team including Barbara Remillard, Sandra Brauner, Bhupendra Kunwar, and Victoria Gazeley – all of whom have made huge contributions to this book and helped us to keep the ball moving forward. They also were key in helping us to edit, re-write and re-organize the content, along with designing the book cover and website. We could not have done this without you.

To our mentors, past employers and clients – who have taught us the importance of building long-term relationships in business, life, and certainly, in love. We have attempted to apply all of these marketing and sales principles toward finding love after 40!

"Coming together is a beginning. Keeping together is progress. Working together is success." Henry Ford

Introduction

Congratulations on picking up *Dating Success After 40* and embarking on an amazing journey of self-discovery and love. It takes courage and bravery to put yourself out there in the big wide world of dating — especially at mid-life and beyond. We get it! We get you!

Here's some great news for you to think about. Today, there are more single people over the age of 40 than ever before. There are 54 million single people in the U.S. alone. That's right, so hold off on your myriad of excuses about how few people are really available.

There is a plethora of single people waiting for you to meet them, and many of them are probably in your back yard, or right under your nose.

The fact that you've picked up this book and have started reading is a great sign that you're ready to start down the road of dating, once again. We want to help you every step of the way.

We know you're afraid. We feel your pain. We each have experienced the highs and lows of long-term marriages (18+ years) and understand the heartbreak of dissolving relationships.

We also understand that what you're facing is a process of "getting out there" into the dating scene, possibly after decades —as was the situation for each of us—and it can be daunting.

What can we say, but - we're here to help. We will help you navigate the online (and offline) dating landscape that, trust us, is nothing like what you've experienced in the past. Fasten your seat belt, because it's sure to be a sometimes bumpy, thrilling and, ultimately, a joy ride.

Thankfully, we live in the Information Age and are able to access numerous ways to connect with people, near and far. Although nothing can replace that ultimate face-to-face connection with someone, we are now blessed with the availability of tapping into networks of people who are just like us: mid-life and looking for love, companionship, friendship . . . and/or "The One."

Online dating is an amazing venue enabling you to search for the one you like - who may be the one you love - in a much more efficient and productive manner than you could've done in earlier days. Among its many advantages are:

- Accessibility to large numbers of single people
- Commonality and shared interests
- Close geographic region (if you prefer)
- Physical traits you desire (or don't) you can "see" before you meet
- Viewing others in the comfort of your own home or office, *prior* to a face-to-face meeting

We want you to know that you're not alone. In fact, there's a designated week for us— Unmarried and Single Americans Week — every September. That's right, the

Buckeye Singles Council "National Singles Week" was established in Ohio in the 1980s to celebrate single life and recognize singles and their contributions to society. The celebration is for all unmarried people, including those who were never married, or are widowed or divorced, unless otherwise noted.

Get a load of these staggering statistics from the US Census Bureau

There were 102 million unmarried people in America, 18 and older, in 2011. This group comprised 44.1 percent of all U.S. residents 18 and older.*

Fifty three percent of unmarried U.S. residents 18 and older were women in 2011; 47 percent were men.*

Sixty two percent of unmarried U.S. residents, 18 and older in 2011, had never been married. Another 24 percent were divorced, and 14 percent were widowed.*

Seventeen million unmarried U.S. residents were 65 and older in 2011. These seniors comprised 16 percent of all unmarried people 18 and older.*

There are 89 unmarried men 18 and older for every 100 unmarried women in the United States in 2011.*

Fifty five million households were maintained by unmarried men and women in 2011. These households comprised 46 percent of households nationwide.**

Thirty three million people lived alone in 2011. They comprised 28 percent of all households, up from 17 percent in 1970.***

* Source: America's Families and Living Arrangements: 2011<http://www.census.gov/population/www/socdemo/ hh-fam/cps2011.html> Table A1.

** Source: America's Families and Living Arrangements: 2011?<http://www.census.gov/population/www/socdemo/ hh-fam/cps2011.html> Table A2

*** *Source: America's Families and Living Arrangements: 2011?<http://www.census.gov/population/www/socdemo/ hh-fam/cps2011.html> Table H1 and HH-*

The numbers of single people looking for love online are staggering. There are more than 40 million people who have enrolled with online dating sites.

We both admit, contemplating going "online" to find true love seemed awkward and forced . . . at first. However, what are two recently single mid-lifers supposed to do when nearly all of our friends are married, know relatively few single people (if any) who might be potential "matches" for us, and might be unlikely to make an introduction, regardless?

Not only were our married friends hesitant to make introductions, but we were uncomfortable to ask them to, in case it might not work out. That would be, ah . . . awkward. We already were feeling like we were reliving our puberty—yet here we were, already middle aged, and found ourselves faced with dating after years of being off the market.

Also, in each of our cases - we were living in the burbs so as not to disrupt our kids' education and their teenage social life (trust us, they were having a lot more fun socially than we were when we began this journey). We also remember being frequently reminded, "no one is going to knock on your door and ask you out."

True enough.

So, what were we to do? Sit home weekend after weekend when all of our married friends were with their family and we were home alone, or watching repeats of

HGTV on Saturday nights? (Well, that's what Nancy was doing for many consecutive weekends).

Walking the beach and going to yoga classes all weekend was fine alone, but sure would be more enjoyable with the love of our life by our side. So we did what any other single guy and gal would do — contemplated marketing ourselves to the masses of other singles in our preferred age ranges, personal preferences, and interests, and get out there - online.

Having come from marketing (Nancy) and sales (Neil) backgrounds, we each individually set about promoting and selling ourselves online. We know, you might be thinking: "Really, I have to sell myself to someone?" We say, "Absolutely, you do, and when you do, your chances for success in love will be increased ten-fold."

If at this point you aren't willing to think of yourself as an individual who needs to market yourself online, that's understandable - who would? Luckily for us, we didn't have any trouble wrapping our minds around this notion. That's because we were professionally trained— through our educational experience and on-the-job learning in our own businesses— in marketing and sales strategies, as basic requirements to earn a living. Why not apply them to our quests of finding a match online?

We met through a mutual friend, Mark Magnacca, who thought we'd have something in common professionally, as well as both having a sincere interest in marketing and selling oneself on a more personal level through dating on- and off-line. A "marriage" was born after Nancy heard Neil speak on the topic of online dating. A meeting ensued, and as they say - the rest is history.

We came together to share our individual and

respective insights on dating and finding true love - as well as to apply our collective knowledge of marketing and sales strategies to the dating game. In many ways, it is a "game" that you should have fun with and enjoy the process of playing. All too often, we discount the journey for what's at the finish line. That's a shame, because this experience has so much to offer us in terms of meeting new people, having new experiences and making new friendships, regardless of whether it ends in true love.

So, there may be some skeptics out there who feel that "marketing" or "selling" yourself to find a mate is somehow inauthentic or forced. We strongly disagree, and we'll tell you why: We all "buy" based on our desires for something (or someone). It may seem unromantic on the surface, but we all tend to "position" ourselves for success - in our businesses, on the job, in our relationships with family members and colleagues, and when searching for a potential partner or lover. Why not?

Throughout the book, you'll be exposed to marketing and sales lingo that we'll define and explain how it specifically relates to dating and finding an ideal match. We promise to keep it simple and straightforward, and explain as we move through each chapter. Using sales and marketing analogies is what makes this book unique.

No other dating book, we are aware of, is using these basic selling techniques to find true love. We know firsthand how this works in each of our businesses, as well as how well it has worked as we embarked on a new adventure of online dating. We want nothing more than to share these tips, strategies and tactics with you.

Many of you will be, or have been, making up excuses as to why you can't date . . . yet. Your kids are too young, you're working too hard, you have no time, it's overwhelming, there are no good men/women out there, they're all married, the single ones are jerks, I don't have enough money to be in a relationship, etc., etc., etc.

We understand the millions of reasons why people come up with excuses not to be their happiest and best selves in a relationship with someone they love. Many of these "excuses," we realize, are legitimate. Many are not, and are the "reasons" that keep us held back. Fear (of failure - or success) can create gridlock on the relationship and love front. That's not what we want for you.

We came together to write this book to be your dating "coaches" and help you enjoy the process of getting to know others who have at least one thing in common (and probably many more)— they're single and looking for a relationship—just like you are.

Both of us are passionate about helping you to find that person who will contribute to your life, share your interests and help to bring joy and happiness you might have been lacking without this special someone.

We both love our individual businesses and what they can provide to our respective customer bases, in both our marketing and sales practices. However, our passion is in helping others to find the love in their lives with another individual.

Very few people, at the end of their lives, wish they had worked another day, taken on a new client or completed that last project. They always wish they had spent more time enjoying the people in their lives. Don't waste another second "waiting" for that man or woman to enter your life to enhance your experience today. Start now, while you're alive and well.

No doubt, you'll learn much about yourself, human nature, new ways of behaving in relationships and how marketing and sales strategies can increase your chances of finding love on and offline. If you're single right now and don't want to be, you've got nothing to lose by reading this book and culling from it what resonates with you.

We are not therapists, but are true practitioners of having walked in your shoes. Our advice and coaching is based on our individual and collective experience of dating as grown-ups in a new and fast-paced world using the Internet. We'll also go beyond online dating and walk you through the first date, follow-up dates, and help you know when to say, "deal" or "no deal" without burning any bridges or acting unkindly.

Look at this process as an incredible opportunity to expand your social network, make new friends, meet new people and create a more fulfilling life for yourself through relationships with people you haven't even met yet. Now, that's exciting!

Chapter 1

Why Online Dating is a
Marketing and Sales Job

In 1986—over a quarter of a century ago— *Newsweek* magazine made an astounding cover story claim that shocked the nation and took on a life of its own. The claim? College-educated, single women over 40 had a better chance of getting killed by a terrorist than finding a husband.

Headlines like this (even in the pre-9/11 world) of "killed by a terrorist" proved titillating to the American press. Because media builds upon itself, this subject went viral and instilled fear among single women of all ages who were looking for love. It was even quoted in Nora Ephron's 1993 movie, *Sleepless in Seattle*. What *Newsweek* failed to mention, however, is that the authors of the study they were reporting on never actually made that claim. In spite of the researchers' insistence that their data had been misinterpreted, the cat was out of the bag, so to speak.

Newsweek finally did apologize - on June 5th, 2006 - 20 years after their "mistake" of running this cover story.

Although this anecdote merely confirms what you

probably already knew—that you can't believe every-thing you see and read in newspapers, magazines, online, or other forms of media including blogs, social media, etc.— still, whether you're a single woman or a single man, it may be prudent to take a pro-active stance on your dating opportunities.

Personally, as avid marketers and salespeople, we believe you need to start thinking of yourself as a product or service that needs to be packaged, marketed and sold. We know, we know - it sounds so unromantic and "stra-tegic," but it's a valid, tested approach which we guaran-tee will provide more success than thinking your Prince or Princess Charming will seek you out, find you and presto! You'll live together happily ever after (and all this accomplished with very little effort).

Sure, love and romance sells. We get it. We too wanted it, and we went after it, each of us in our own way. Our only advantage over most of you reading this book is that we were trained to think like a marketer and a sales-person. Now we want to share our strategies and secrets with you - hence the birth of this authoring partnership: Nancy and Neil.

Throughout the book, we'll give you our "take" on the dating world, and how to navigate it, both off and online.

We're going to tackle this task as a marketing and sales "project." Finding true love is a process where - just as in marketing and sales - you need to create the "know, like, trust factor" among your prospects (potential dates or mates).

How is this done successfully, and with a minimum of pain and a maximum of pleasure? We will cover a myriad of ways to meet your match, throughout ***Dating Success after 40***.

Both of us have been in a situation similar to where you may find yourself right now— perhaps experiencing a separation, divorce, thrust back into the dating game, etc. — and it all hasn't been so pretty. We've also gone on our share of "challenging" dates that were not so much fun, but necessary to help determine, and get more clear on, what we actually were looking for.

So, mostly we'll be talking to you as a team of two professionals speaking in one voice. Occasionally, though, one of us wants to share a personal point of view, such as when Nancy wants to speak directly to you ladies, or when we two simply disagree on a point. When that happens, we break out of the partnership mold. In fact, there's an example of that coming up here and now:

NANCY: Here's something we disagree on: I am a believer that the opportunity to "land a man" is a matter of a nanosecond, whereas Neil....well, let's just listen in to what he confessed (unknowingly) in a recent meeting. Neil explained that he had been contacted by two women he had corresponded with, prior to finding true love with - let's call her "L." Names will be withheld to protect the innocent/guilty here. You get it, right?

Apparently, a few weeks had gone by and Neil had already committed himself to L, and had removed his profile from Match.com. Alas, two interested parties sought him out after realizing he had taken his profile down. His response was that "I wish you had reached out sooner, we have a lot in common and I would have liked to get to know you." Now, however, he was committed to L and was no longer online seeking relationships.

Ladies, this is why it's even more important for us to put our marketing and sales hat on and act when the spirit moves us. In my humble opinion, women can do better alone - than most men can do. Here's the other killer (according to me- Neil wants to insist that you all know this opinion is coming from me only): women, as they age, have an increasingly more "challenging" time with dating, whether online or offline.

I was relatively new to the dating scene when I picked up the phone and called Patti Stanger - you know, the "hostess with the most-ess" of Millionaire Matchmaker on the Bravo network. I was 43 at the time when Patti "suggested" or "told" me to be looking in the 50 or 60-something store. Translation? Men your own age will be less interested than a more "mature" man, who will think that "you're the bomb" - being the "younger woman" with the older man. As it turns out, most of my "significant others" have averaged around 10 years my senior. I claim I'm just super "mature." Neil begs to differ.

I'm all for dating and being with a younger man, but so far - not happenin'.

Side note: If you fit this description, please call . . .

Just kidding. We're here to help YOU!

Here's another thought. Women are used to relying on friends, family, coworkers, children, colleagues and . . . well, others for emotional support. I know, this is a gross generalization, but men tend to need a woman in their life more quickly than most women need a man in theirs.

That just makes our job as women a bit more challenging, which is why having a good sense of marketing and sales will be so important in this process.

For all of us, men and women alike, our job is to show up (Woody Allen said that 80 percent of success is in showing up), put our best image forward (in person and online), reach out (let people know you're interested in meeting someone) and persistence - in the words of Eleanor Roosevelt, "never, never, never give up."

Sure, it's a challenge to find love at any age and stage of life, but know this: it can be done, and it is happening every day of the week. Get your head in the game and open your mouth to those you know already, to tell them you're interested in dating. Get online and write a killer profile (we'll help you with that in Chapter 5). Get out of town and do something you're interested in that gives you pleasure - with or without someone by your side. Chances are, if you're taking care of your needs and having a good time while doing so - people will take note.

We know from experience that there's no bigger or better turn-on than seeing someone who's optimistic and who enjoys meeting new people, doing new things and taking advantage (in a good way) of all that life has to offer. Don't sit on the sidelines (or locked inside your home) and expect the world to come to you. You've got to take consistent action to create opportunities to meet that special someone, who is just waiting for you to appear.

Here's another thing. Don't let the statistics get you down. For every "sad" story out there, there are 10 amazing scenarios of true love being found online - a medium that only in the past decade has become a viable way of connecting with people, through friends and family, outside activities and personal interests, etc.

As human beings, both men and women have age range preferences that run the gamut. We say, whatever turns you on is OK. Just understand what's going on and never give up reaching out to those you find interesting - either at online dating sites or seeing the sights around town. The truth is, you never know who will be an ideal match or where, or how, you'll meet them.

Dating is about reach and frequency (another marketing term). You need to be out there on a regular basis in order to meet someone. You may need to step out of your comfort zone (another semi-marketing/sales term) to put yourself out there and let others know you're interested in a relationship. Unless your friends, relatives, neighbors and colleagues are psychic, they may not know these things.

Some of us will prefer to do our "searches" in the comfort of our own home or office - online, and others are more hands-on, wanting to volunteer in the community, take a cooking class, or telling friends and family that they're ready, willing and able to start dating again. A marketing mix is the ideal way to find a potential mate, and spreading the word in the way(s) you're most comfortable will most likely lead to success.

Throughout *Dating Success after 40*, we will refer to marketing and sales terminology, tactics and strategies you can reference and, hopefully, relate to your quest to find the ideal man or woman. At a minimum, we know if you keep an open heart and open mind, you'll end up with new friends you might never before have had the opportunity or the good fortune to meet.

NANCY: On my first Match.com date, I met a wonderful younger man (I know - you're doing the math on my average date's age - don't go there). Let's call him "P" - eeuw - "P" doesn't sound nearly as good as Neil's "L," does it? Anyhow, P made it clear early on he was looking for love and marriage. At the time, I was well on my way to divorce court, but was nowhere near being ready to contemplate marriage. P was ready - at 39 and single, he wanted a legally committed relationship (our word these days for "marriage") and all that went with it.

In the end, the relationship wasn't viable, but even after it was over -we've remained friends, and P was the one male friend who, when I fell seriously ill, brought my kids to visit me in the hospital. Since then, we've gone on to be great friends, and recently, my significant other and I had the pleasure of attending his wedding. I've also written a recommendation to the adoption agency I used for my two Chinese daughters' adoptions, on behalf of P and his wife, "C."

We hope your head isn't spinning already, as it's our job to give it to you straight up (with a twist) - and it's our intent to make this process a fun one for you. Think of this as an adventure you're about to embark on with two completely objective friends who have your best interest at heart. We promise not to make this experience overwhelming; however, we will make it both comprehensive and a "how-to manual" that we both definitely wish we had had before venturing out on our own in the dating world.

Fortunately for you, we've been through the school of hard knocks and can provide you with our collective experience, now turned into useful knowledge, about the most efficient ways of mind mapping the dating scene post-40. That's our job and we take it seriously, but with a big sense of humor too!

We will also be introducing you to several experts in their respective fields, who will offer you the trade secrets they share with their clients.

Kimberly Seltzer, of **Elite Image Makeovers**, is one such expert, and she was kind enough to share the following:

Once upon a time I had a pretty traditional life: a husband, two beautiful children, a dog and a suburban house with a white picket fence - until I was blindsided with divorce. I suddenly found myself a single mom trying to uncover who I was again, separate from my husband, and was catapulted back into this thing called "dating." I had a closet full of oversized black "mommy" tops, a bunch of nursing bras and Birkenstock sandals. Not a very appealing image.

More importantly, I wasn't feeling attractive, and I didn't know how to give signals that I was even interested in men. The last date I remembered having was going to a toga fraternity party in college. Boy, were things different now! I didn't know if I would ever get my groove back and feel like a sexy, charming and dateable woman again. This is where my journey began and it's why I became a dating and makeover expert, so I could help people rediscover who they are, gain confidence and attract love.

Whether you have been married before or not, feeling secure when it comes to dating after 40 is easier said than done. People expect that dating is going to be the same as it was when they were in their early 20s, and it's not at all. The dating pool is different, and people have different life circumstances and stressors to contend with.

Another problem when you are coming out of a divorce or long relationship is that your identity has been linked with your ex-partner for so long that you forget who you are separate from that person. Other challenges can be: dealing with the emotional turmoil of divorce, the responsibility of raising children and keeping up with the demands of finances and your job. You are forced to wear many hats and juggle schedules - all the while attempting to look good and date!

Despite its challenges, if you feel good about yourself and know what you want, finding love and dating can be fun. It takes time and patience, but there are a few things you can do to get started and regain some of those dating skills that may have gotten rusty.

The first step is to get back to the basics - YOU!

Change Your Mindset And Focus On You

Focus on figuring out what your passions are to really get in touch with your true self. Dating can be overwhelming, so focus on you first. After being in a long-term relationship, people tend to stop doing what they used to love. Revisit the things that once inspired you and get involved again. Perhaps there are hobbies, places to travel or extra-curricular activities that you've wanted to do. Reconnecting with your passions will help you find the things that make you happy, focus on yourself and even meet other likeminded single people.

Also, after divorce or a long relationship, many people try to numb the pain by quickly getting involved with someone else. That, however, is just a Band-Aid over a wound that needs time to heal. Slow down and don't worry about getting into another relationship right away. Think of it this way - if you're running a marathon you can't sprint the whole way. You'll get hurt and fall short. Instead, pace yourself. Make eye contact and smile at people who are noticing you. Create an energy that invites people towards you. Keep putting one foot in front of the other and soon you will be on your way and enjoying the journey.

Chapter 2

Looking Back to Move Forward

Nobody likes a victim or a martyr—nor does anybody want to listen to someone's hours-long monologue about how "bad" their ex is. Really. Trust us, we know. Think about it: now that you're starting a new chapter in your life, your attitude should reflect that.

We all have a story, and it usually is complicated. After all, you don't get to be post-40 and not have encountered relationship drama along the way. While there is no hard and fast rule about when it's appropriate to date after a break-up or loss of a partner, it is definitely a necessity to heal those past hurts before you can move forward.

If you don't do that, you're likely to repel your dates by giving the impression that you're unhappy, stuck in the past, and may turn out to be a lot of work for them if they choose to get involved. This is not the message you want to be sending!

NANCY: Sometimes the body needs both emotional and physical healing, as was the case in my situation.

I was age 41 when my husband of 16 years told me he wanted out. I was left with three small children (two girls adopted from China and a surprise biological son with Asperger's, who came between the two adoptions) and the stress of running my business and managing my home….. alone.

I soon became ill but ignored the warning signs, as I continued to keep life as normal as possible for my children. Eventually, my body would not be silenced, and I underwent an emergency liver transplant in May 2005, due to a virus that attacked my organs.

The weeks leading up to that fateful day had been a combination of extreme fatigue, vomiting, and weakness, but I was determined to fulfill my business obligations, assuming it was just the flu. It all came to a head when I literally could not walk off the plane that brought me home from a speaking engagement in Atlantic City. A friend picked me up and drove me to my local ER and the following day I was transported to Beth Israel Deaconess Medical Center (BIDMC) in Boston.

I was admitted to the Intensive Care Unit, where I stayed for three months, two of which I spent in a coma after the liver transplant. I coded twice during the surgery and the doctors attempted to prepare my parents for the worst. Within two weeks of my surgery, I had a routine brain scan for the opening they had to drill in my head to alleviate cranial pressure. There was an abscess and I underwent emergency brain surgery, all the while in a coma. The doctors were very worried about brain damage.

When I awoke two months later, I found that I had a tube inserted in my windpipe and could not speak — very frightening! The realization of what had happened was overwhelmingly confusing and I didn't have my voice — literally and figuratively.

Nonetheless, my ex continued with divorce proceedings and instituted a petition to obtain custody of my three children, since I was unable to care for them.

Fast forward: my recovery took about two full years

because of the extensive rehabilitation necessitated by my having lost 1/3 of my body weight, my strength, etc.

Bottom line is, I'm here today — back with my three children, have re-launched my business, and am happily involved in a long-term relationship.

The short story is, I am the most fortunate person I know, because I not only survived but am now thriving. However, had I not taken the time to get healthy, heal my body and my mind, I would not have had anything to offer a potential mate. A relationship is a two-way street. If you're not coming into it with a healthy mind and body, it will be DOA before it even begins.

I never talk about this straight out of the gate with someone. There's no doubt in my mind that they too have their sad story to tell, and sometimes having some time and space to get to know someone before embarking on the "who done somebody wrong song" is a welcome relief. Otherwise, that song can be the biggest turn-off to people, so beware of airing your dirty laundry too soon.

NEIL: My story is quite different, but nevertheless, I totally agree that recovery of body and spirit are absolutely essential before you can move on and find love again. I only had to recover from a heart that fell out of love and a long-term marriage that dissolved. The fire had died and neither of us was at fault. Actually, I admit that I fell out of love in the marriage. Although we were both faithful, the wonderful spark we once had was finally reduced to a cold ember.

After moving out of our home and into my own place, it took me time to analyze what I wanted in a relationship and the type of woman I wanted to be with. I read *Eat, Pray, Love* and that helped me tremendously! I also came to realize what I did not want in a relationship, and that's just as important to understand as what you do want. I looked at my baggage of past relationships, fixed what needed to be fixed and then felt comfortable moving on. Today, I feel so much better and look forward to a loving and wonderful relationship.

We are so thrilled to have **Cija Black**, author of *Modern Love: The Grownup's Guide to Relationships & Online Dating* and creator of the online Udemy class: *Sorting Your Love Baggage,* give some much-needed advice to those of us who are singing the "somebody done somebody wrong song." Cija stresses the importance of leaving behind past hurt, emotions, anger and sometimes rage we might have toward our ex.

We hope you pay special attention to what Cija offers, and we know if you implement her advice, your dates will be happy you did. Here's what she has written especially for this book:

So there you are, lit only by the computer screen, ready to write your dating profile. But, do you really know what you're looking for in a mate?

There are some things I encourage you to consider before diving into the dating pool. Doing so will help you have a much more successful dating experience. I encourage you to take a look at your past relationships and dig through some of that love baggage to see what's in there. Going through this process will help you unearth your expectations and hopes for how you assume love should be. There may be some old ways of thinking that no longer serve you.

Why Is Your Baggage So Heavy?

Dictionary.com defines **baggage** as:

"*Things that encumber one's freedom, progress, development, or adaptability; impediments: intellectual baggage that keeps one from thinking clearly; neurotic conflicts that arise from struggling with too much emotional baggage.*" (http://www.dictionary.com/)

With words like "encumber," "impediment" and "neurotic conflicts," it's easy to see why your baggage can feel so heavy and overwhelming. It's extra mental "stuff" that you're carrying around and it's getting in the way of your ability to make progress. It's a lot easier to move around your emotional space when you take stock of what baggage you have, understand why you have it, and then determine whether you really still need it. You are not defined by what has happened in your life unless you choose to be. As we move along in our lives we evolve, change and grow, and can define who we are for ourselves.

But first we must recognize events and behaviors as just that, and not as a definition of who we are as a person. Commit to taking charge of your life; you are the only person with the power, right and responsibility to define You. Does your baggage from the past still serve the current you?

Baggage can take many forms, but for the purposes of this discussion we are going to tackle the kind filled with the stories, hurts and patterns from your romantic relationships.

What Your Past Can Teach You About Your Now

Our first model for adult romantic relationships is

generally our parents, parental figures, and/or other family we are surrounded by as children. As we grow up we collect these experiences in our memory and process them through our own unique filters. These filters can result in both good and bad messages and behaviors that we play out as adults.

Odds are that since you've made it this far in your life, you have a dating and relationship history of some sort and have built up a set of assumptions and expectations that govern how relationships should work. Even if you haven't had many relationships or related experiences, you will probably still have developed a set of expectations for how relationships are "supposed" to be.

Regardless of how your relationship expectations have evolved, you know you probably have room for improvement. Your collected assumptions and habits about relationships are like those junk drawers in your kitchen where you throw in all that stuff you don't want to deal with. It's time to do some spring cleaning: keep and polish the best stuff, toss the useless and outdated, and make some space for some sparkly new dating tools and relationship ideas.

We are not going to relive the painful memories, or ride the old roller coaster; we are not going to judge you as a winner or loser. What we are going to do is look at your patterns objectively. Only you know all the stories and why you made the choices you did. This is not an exercise in blaming yourself; it's a lesson in understanding your own personal "why" — and also to see if those "whys" still apply to who you are now.

The End

We're going to begin at The End. That's where you are right now. This is where life and love have brought you, right to this very moment, reading this book. What's exciting about The End is that you get the benefit of all that life experience. You're no longer a 15-year old gawky kid who's unsure of everything. You're ahead of the curve in your own life.

Most of us are so caught up in where we are going we don't pause to review where we have been. That being said, you now need to sort through some of these past experiences and consider what you liked, what you didn't and — most importantly — understand why you had those positive and negative responses to this series of life events. Once you sort through these pieces you can determine how you would like to improve your future experiences in the game of love.

There are good and bad things that have occurred in everyone's life, and even the bad things are worth taking note of. Taking the time to carefully consider those less than stellar moments and situations allows you to gain some insight and adjust course where appropriate. As you assimilate this information and move forward, you'll be better equipped to deal with new experiences. The very best part about endings is that a new beginning is right around the corner.

The other great thing about endings is that you get to insert a new phrase into your life: "I used to." Whenever you catch yourself describing something as "always" happening to me," you get to replace that "always" with a past tense of "that used to" happen to me. Repeat after me: "<insert issue here> used to happen to me." This allows you to strengthen your definition of who you are now and clearly delineate that from the old you.

The lessons from your past tend to be more easily understood in hindsight; you just have to be sure you recognize and categorize accordingly. One of the biggest obstacles that hold people back from really living their best life is that they don't stop to give themselves credit for how far they have come. We learn from the failures as well as the successes. Take a moment to reflect, and give yourself a pat on the back. You've been through some battles, and had some triumphs as well, and they all made you the person you are right now.

Now is the time to reinvent yourself. This is YOUR life, where you get to be the best you, where you get to keep what works for you, tweak and improve what you like best and leave behind what doesn't work, as often as you'd like.

Give yourself permission to define and redefine who you are, and never, ever give that power and control to someone else. True freedom comes when you give yourself permission and accept the responsibility to define what you like, whom you like and what you choose to do with your life.

So, take a breath and savor this moment. Let go of those limiting "always" situations and file them under "used to." Release those old fears; they were useful once, but you have exciting new experiences awaiting you.

How Exactly Does "Happily Ever After" Work?
Many of us spend our lives looking for that perfect person, that special someone to "complete" us. Odds are if you grew up in the United States in the 1980s,

you were stuffed full of popular fairytales and teenage angst films.

The formula went something like this: through a series of awkward events and dramatic moments, a magical person would appear in your life at just the right moment; generally in the middle of some major crisis like a prom or shortly after you lost your glass slipper. Once this prince/princess/savior found you, they would proceed to fall deeply in love with you, solve all of your problems and you would then, quite effortlessly, live happily ever after (complete with ribbon-carrying birds encircling your love).

If you bought any part of the fairy tale even secretly, you might be a bit miffed that this scenario hasn't played out for you yet. You might not even be aware that you have been using that "perfect-complete-me" set of standards. Or, even worse, you were duped into a relationship with someone who 'fit' the formula, only to realize that you were both real people under those fairytale costumes and expectations— and that "happily ever after" was much more complicated then you thought.

It's not surprising that you have some of these hopes, especially when you're beaten over the head with these messages over and over again. The repetition of this information is bound to register somewhere in your skull as some form of "truth." Don't feel bad if you bought into this myth — many of us did. It's good to know where your expectations for romance and relationships come from and simply recognize that you have them. Knowing they are there and how they got there is half the battle. We all bought into it to some degree, but we now know better, don't we! It's now time to revamp your expectations, so you can get on with the business of enjoying your **real** life with your **real** partner!

Unlike in fairy tales, people have flaws, life is messy and relationships take a lot more work than fairy tales led us to believe. How many of your romantic expectations are based on television shows, pop songs or movies you saw growing up? Romantic fiction in any of those forms is a disappointing standard to hold yourself or your partner to. Especially if you don't communicate those standards openly! What goes on in "happily ever after" anyway?

The good news is that in place of the perfect partner and effortless relationship, there is something much better and far more realistic in store for you. You can, and should have standards for the partners and romantic relationships in your life, but they should be based on criteria you consciously create. If you're willing to hold yourself to certain standards and not settle for the next warm body, you will improve the quality of your dating prospects immensely. No one is perfect, there is no "perfect" love, and relationships do take work; particularly the good ones.

Ideals, Standards and Boundaries

To be clear, the "Ideal" in terms of love is not an inflexible fantasy, an unreasonable set of expectations, or the movie-perfect "happily ever after." Rather, it's a goal that helps you define the path to get you where you want to go.

Your own personal standards and boundaries work together to create a path and structure to help you reach the goal of your ideal. We often talk of the ideal partner and relationship for us; the perfect guy or girl. When you clearly define your Ideal you, partner and relationship, you are then able to clarify the standards and boundaries you need to get you there.

Your Ideal is what you are aiming yourself towards; it's your direction and personal map. Your standards are the lines painted on the highway of your life, and are enforced by the boundaries that clearly define what is OK, and what is unacceptable in your life. They provide the structure that gets you closer to your Ideal. The clearer you are about these standards the easier it is to say "No" without feeling guilty, and the easier it is to say "yes" when things are going right! That's because you know what it will take to get you to your ideal.

Your boundaries enforce your standards with the people in your life. In order to maintain a quality relationship you must clearly define your own boundaries and respect the boundaries of others. A partner can't meet a standard or boundary they don't know about, and neither can you, so clarifying these is a critical piece of communication in a relationship. Otherwise you are both stumbling through an emotional minefield, landing on hot buttons and issues you didn't even know existed.

What You Learn From Your Family

What you learned as a child through watching the people in your life formed your foundation for how you think relationships work. As a child, you're a human sponge; you absorb it all. You take in everything you see and experience and put feelings and meanings to that input. Some things have words put to them, some are just feelings. That's how you learn and grow. We each had our own unique family experience that helped shape our sense of trust, love, relationship and safety. Those seeds are planted in you when you are a child, and you grow and carry those concepts with you throughout your life.

On top of this input during childhood, add the romantic relationships you observed as a child. As you get older and delve into romantic love yourself, you take all that knowledge and will do a number of things with it. You might copy the patterns you've grown up with; you may do the opposite of what you grew up with. Or you might fall somewhere in the middle and embrace some behaviors and disregard others. Regardless of the path you choose, you will probably adjust your approach throughout your life.

The imprint of my parents' relationship and how it impacted the way I viewed romantic relationships came to light late in my own marriage. I found that up until that point, I was very strong-willed and extremely independent. When I got married, however, somewhere in the baggage I'd collected as a child, I thought I was supposed to behave differently as a wife. "Wife" meant I could not be as overtly strong, self-focused and confident as I had been, and that my husband should come first.

That definition was so deeply embedded in my brain that I wasn't even aware that it was modifying my behavior and personality until the end of my marriage. After my divorce and some breathing room, it became clear how my acceptance of that definition had made a profoundly negative impact on my marriage.

Each of us has in our head certain ideas tied to relationship status - in my case it was marriage. Each of these relationship types comes with permissions, expectations, requirements, and in extreme cases, shackles. We find ourselves living by these guidelines whether we're consciously aware of them or not.

The particular definitions you apply to a relationship status and/or roles are unique to you. It's up to you to figure out what they are and decide whether you'd like to keep them once you've identified them. Later in this chapter, you'll find a series of questions that will help to do just that.

Those expectations go both ways; you have yours and your partner has his or hers. Remember the lesson above - never make assumptions that your partner defines things the way you do. The way you define a relationship status or role may differ **greatly** from the way your partner defines that same status or role. If you've ever found yourself disappointed at your partner's response or reaction, there's a strong likelihood that your relationship definitions and expectations were at play and that they don't match up with your partner's.

Having expectations and definitions is natural; you'll both have them. The key is sharing and communicating them, so that you can resolve differences and head off potential issues, before they become real problems.

Considering Where You Have Been

How do you feel about the partners you've had in the past? Do you lump them all in the category of "loser," or were there some good ones in the bunch? Review those past players and see what the similarities and differences are between them. What are the qualities from past partners that you want to keep and what do you want to pitch? What is your pattern of picking partners? Often it's easier to see the patterns in your life when you think about yourself in the context of particular relationships.

Think back to a particularly good or bad relationship and how it impacted your behavior and your life. Do you recall friends saying you seemed happy, distracted, agitated, stressed, upset, etc. when you were in particular relationships? Pull out your old journals, photos and letters from the past. It might be painful to do this, but it's a good way to see your past and experiences from a new and clearer vantage point. When you consider memories from your past, what were the constants in your life? What was missing? Visiting your past can give you powerful insight into your patterns, strengths and weaknesses and can help you move forward in a positive way.

This process may dredge up strong emotions. Remember that you survived, and that these are only memories. Take this opportunity to review your past relationships; from this vantage point they won't be so charged. Doing this gives you the chance to clear out old emotional baggage and also make way for new relationships.

"My Crap, Your Crap" - Separating Your Issues From Your Partner's

The heat of the moment is the hardest time to control your emotions, communicate your needs and hold to your defenses, but it is also the most important moment to make the choice to respond differently for good. By doing this work now, the next time someone bumps into one of your boundaries, you will have a clear idea of why you respond the way you do, and you will have the choice to respond differently next time.

When you start a relationship you spend time together and interact; you do your thing and they do theirs. Interacting with another person sets off a series of actions, reactions and responses from each of you. The reactions are formulated by your own life experiences. You will find that your response to particular situations may be entirely different from that of your partner's and this can be a shock. This is something I like to call "My Crap, Your Crap." Basically, this means that you come into the relationship with your experiences ("My Crap") and so does your partner ("Your Crap"). When you and your partner find yourself having a disagreement, you need to put it through the "My Crap, Your Crap" filter. You need to figure out what category your disagreement falls under:

- **It's coming up because of something from your past,** long before this person arrived in your life. This is likely an old boundary that you have had violated too many times in the past.
- **It's coming up because of something from your partner's past**, long before you arrived in his or her life. It is a boundary that they had to defend in the past.
- **It's your collective problem as a couple** and something for both of you to work through. This could be due to culture shock and different backgrounds clashing.

You each enter the relationship with a lifetime of experiences, assumptions and the baggage that comes with all of that. When you come together in this particular relationship, you are combining those two sets of life experiences and "results may vary." Hopefully, the mix is mostly good, and usually in the beginning it's easier to glide over misunderstandings. But it's rarely perfect and it will most likely require adjustment on both your parts.

When you find yourself having a disagreement with

your partner or recall disagreements from the past, allow yourself to take a moment and really think about the situation. You may find that the response you had to a particular situation actually has nothing to do with your current partner but rather with something or someone from the past.

If you are willing to step back and see it for what it is —something to be acknowledged, sorted through and most importantly not taken out on your current relationship or the new partner — you stand a much better chance of having a healthy relationship. The issues you have with past relationships are important lessons learned that can help you to create healthy boundaries without emotional bruises.

Realize, however, that not all knee-jerk reactions and land mines are meant to be carried forward — at least not with the same force — with new and unsuspecting partners. What was an important boundary with one person may not even be necessary with the new one.

The upshot of all of this is that you both come into the relationship as individuals, complete with your own series of experiences, issues and expectations. Being aware that your way is not the only way is important for the health of your future relationships. Digging through your past relationships and pulling apart what was really your issues vs. their issues will help you see how you can improve your expectations with potential new matches.

By making an explicit agreement between the two of you when the relationship begins to work together to identify issues, and work through them, you can use those roadblocks to grow and strengthen your relationship.

"The Relationship"

The collection of experiences that you and the other person bring to the table form "The Relationship." This entity is like adding a third personality into the mix. It has a life of its own, consisting of the combined experiences and resulting expectations that the two of you bring. As you've lived your lives, you've gathered up information you've seen in movies, witnessed in your family, heard in songs, experienced in previous relationships etc., and all of these pieces of information have formed the ideas each of you have about how relationships should work. These help you form the rules that govern how each of the players in the relationship is "supposed" to behave.

You will likely find that you each have slightly—or in some cases extremely different— ideas, expectations and rules about the concepts of casual dating, serious relationships and marriage. There are certain rights and rules associated with different relationship statuses, and digging into the questions in the following section will help you understand how you feel about them. The easiest way to uncover those differences is to simply have a conversation between the two of you and ask questions like:

- What does the term "casual relationship" mean to you?
- Do we see each other exclusively?
- Will we meet each other's parents or kids?
- Can I leave a toothbrush at your place?
  …you get the point.

First, define how you feel. Next, never assume that someone else defines things the exact same way you do. All relationships could benefit from the practice of stepping back from a disagreement and making sure that you are using the same definitions with regard to the issue you are arguing about.

Definitions are very important when communicating with anyone, but particularly in love relationships. When you assume that the person you are dating has the exact same definitions of love, commitment, and dating without validating them, can cause serious heartache down the road. Never assume that the way you see and define the world is how everyone else does. Doing that only leads to frustration.

One more time! : Never, ever assume you and your partner share the same definitions on everything. Talk about it! Clear communication is one of the most important elements of a successful relationship, and making sure you are using the same vocabulary will go a long way toward that goal.

Where to Go From Here

The concepts suggested in this section will give you an excellent starting point for clarifying what you are looking for. If you can spend some time sorting that love baggage, you're going to be able to create a strong dating profile that will get you that much closer to finding a romantic connection.

Questions to Ponder

I want to leave you with some questions to consider to help you identify and sort your baggage and define what you're looking for. These questions are meant to get you thinking not only about what you want from a relationship, but why you want those things.

1. Why do you want to date? What do you hope it will bring to your life?
2. Do you change when you're in a relationship? If so, how?
3. What do you do well in a relationship? What do you not do well?
4. How do you handle conflict?
5. How do you expect your relationship to nurture your life?
6. How do you define the following words: relationship, love, dating, casual dating, marriage, dates, boyfriend/girlfriend, partner, date, breakup, romantic, attractive, passionate, independent?
7. Do you have a particular type you are attracted to? Describe that type.
8. How have your past partners nurtured or eroded the relationships you had with them?
9. How did past partners meet or not meet your expectations?
10. What traits would your ideal partner have? Are you OK with flaws? What are your expectations in a relationship?
11. What always seemed to be missing?
12. What would a typical day in your relationship look like? A holiday? A romantic evening?
13. Do you prefer traditional or more modern relationships? Why? Define what that means to you.
14. What ingredients do you want in your relationship?

Define relationship status from the initial meeting through serious commitment. What are you entitled to with each status?

* * *

Cija's information is priceless, in that we need to embrace our past and release it before we bog down a potential future partner with what "was." No new chapters can begin if we're holding on to the lows of our past lives. Release, and live anew!

Chapter 3

Identify Your Ideal Target Market

Love is a subject that has not only been a dominant theme in literature and the arts for thousands of years, but also became a central issue for scientific study since around the mid-20th century.

It turns out that our need for a personal connection with someone is quite "normal" and expected. We all desire to love and be loved. According to famed psychologist Abraham Maslow's Hierarchy of Needs. The idea is that we operate at various levels of having our needs met, working from the bottom up.

Our first level is physiological needs (security, comfort, food), then safety needs (security and comfort), then social needs (love, friendship and status), followed by self-esteem needs (recognition or status, a feeling of being important), and finally by the highest of Maslow's Hierarchy of Needs which is: self-actualization (our ultimate personal goals which vary from one individual to another).

Maslow's Hierarchy of Needs

1. Biological and Physiological needs – air, food, drink, shelter, warmth, sex, sleep.
2. Safety needs – protection from elements, security, order, law, limits, stability, freedom from fear.
3. Social Needs – belongingness, affection and love, - from work group, family, friends, romantic relationships.
4. Esteem needs – achievement, mastery, independence, status, dominance, prestige, self-respect, and respect from others.
5. Self-actualization needs – realizing personal potential, self-fulfillment, seeking personal growth and peak experiences.

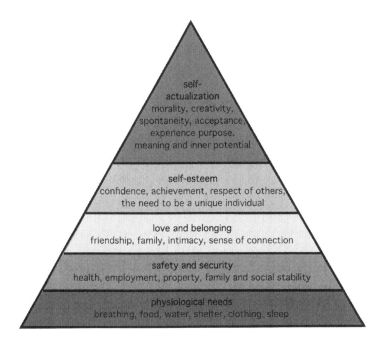

Erik Erikson, another renowned psychologist,

developed the theory that there are Eight Stages of Man. Each stage of a "healthy" developing person should pass from infancy to late adulthood. In each stage of development, an individual confronts and ideally masters new challenges or life stages. Each stage builds upon the successful completion of the earlier stage. If stages are not successfully completed, they may be expected to reappear as challenges in the future.

The good news is that one doesn't have to "master" a particular state to move onto another. Erikson's stage theory is characterized by a psychosocial crisis of two conflicting forces. If an individual does indeed successfully come to terms with these forces (favoring the first mentioned attribute in the crisis), he or she emerges from the stage with the corresponding virtue.

The stage that most fits people like us - single adult people post-40 - is the Psychosocial Stage 6: Intimacy vs. Isolation. The characteristics of this stage include:

- Early adulthood (18 - 40) when people are exploring personal relationships.
- Erikson believed it was vital that people develop close, committed relationships with others. Those who are successful at this step will form relationships that are committed and secure.
- Each step builds on skills learned in previous steps. Erikson believed that a strong sense of personal identity was important for developing intimate relationships. Studies have demonstrated that those with a poor sense of self tend to have less committed relationships and are more likely to suffer emotional isolation, depression and loneliness.
- Successful resolution of this stage results in the virtue

known as love. It is marked by the ability to form lasting, meaningful relationships with other people.

Chances are, by this time in our lives, we have had these experiences of having been in love. The sad news can be that despite our best efforts (or not), lasting love it was not meant to be. Therefore, today we find ourselves seeking out a companion, partner or mate we want to share our life and experiences with. Only now, we're doing this later in the game . . . again. As the saying goes - better late than never. The great news is we probably have a much better idea of what we're looking for and what are potential make it or break it terms of a relationship.

Here's more good news - there are more single people 40+ than ever before in the history of the United States. So, why is it so important to "market" ourselves? Competition is everywhere, people. That doesn't mean it's impossible for us to stand out in a crowd, but some effort will need to be applied. Not to worry. We're here every step of the way with you. Keep the faith and let's get this party started.

We recommend you start out with a list of your "buying criteria." That's right, you are in the buyer's seat when seeking out a partner - so be clear about who and what you want to attract. Keep a written checklist of the ideal attributes you're looking for in a mate.

We all have personal preferences or "types" we are drawn to. There's nothing wrong with that, and the more clear we are on who we are looking for in a partner, the more likely we'll attract that person into our lives. We also have specific interests that we'd like to share with the one we love - hobbies, sporting activities, movies, theatre, cooking, etc. Commit them to paper and refer to your Ideal Partner list as you start this process.

Once you've determined the qualities of your ideal mate, other considerations will, of course, need to be taken into account — and all of this additional information will be will be provided in your online profile (to be discussed in Chapter 5), including demographic "reach." We'll also share our "take" on what you may want to mention and may want to stay away from when we discuss creating your positioning in that chapter. You'll need to think about and quantify what age range you are looking to attract, gender, income range religion, politics, and geographic area.

Susan Winter, best-selling author/relationship expert (*Older Women/Younger Men and Allowing Magnificence*) wrote an interesting piece on how to decide which age bracket you'd like to date, including dating people older or younger than you:

The decisions we make regarding 'age bracket preferences' are based on our past romantic experiences, both positive and negative. If we've had a history of happy relationships with same-aged partners, the tendency is to continue with "what works."

The main reason cited for choosing a same-aged partner is the commonality of "social reference." Having shared the same time period, we understand the socio/political lens through which our mate sees the world. Casual comments about musical groups, TV shows and movies need no explanation. These cohesive factors create a sense of comfort and unity for many couples.

Historically, age brackets were determined by economic factors. The traditional model was that of an older man/younger woman scenario. Power and status was bartered for youth and beauty. The world has changed, and women are now the "new men." Today, we see increasing cases of this role reversal. For mature women who possess their own power and status, the choice is often a younger man. The economic issue of "needing a man" has now shifted to "wanting a man."

Mature women are far more active, independent and empowered than in previous generations. Younger men state their reasons for this romantic preference is that "older women know what they want and don't play games." Having been raised by working moms, younger men see an empowered woman as being attractive rather than threatening (as is the case for many older men).

This new option for love and romance is gaining momentum as both mature women and younger men are able to extend their choices of mate in partnership. The growing trend of younger men actively choosing older female partners is becoming more apparent in society today. Mature women are replicating the historic choices of mature men… because they can. And younger men have no problem being attracted to an older woman who knows her worth.

A willingness to expand beyond our own age bracket can greatly increase the odds of finding someone special. Traditionally the domain of older men seeking younger women, today's modern women are also free to make this choice. And, younger men are now far more open to selecting an older woman as their preferred mate.

Advantages of dating someone younger or older? (energy vs experience and skills in the bedroom)

The advantages of having an older partner are that of the economic stability and the life experience they bring to the relationship. With age comes wisdom. An older partner has "been there." They know the ropes. They can see five moves ahead on the game board of life. An older partner often has greater economic resources and social currency than their younger mate. This can alleviate the couple's financial burden (a known source of partnership conflict.) The younger partner is freed from the burden of economic struggle and able to experience a fuller life with their mate, than on their own. Additional resources provide comfort for both, as they're able to enjoy a greater quality of life together.

The advantages of dating a younger partner are: energy, adventure and discovery. A younger partner still has "fresh eyes." The world has not yet become predictable and commonplace. This is the unique gift a younger mate can offer to an older partner who's become jaded and forgotten that the joy of life rests in a state of "discovery." A younger partner's still learning the ropes and open to seeing life as fresh and fertile. This inherent inspiration allows the older partner to reconnect to a vital life force they may have lost in the pursuit of their career goals and day-to-day living.

In the bedroom

The general assumption has been that the older partner possesses greater skills in the bedroom. Having researched older women/younger men pairings, it's often the case that the younger man has far more sexual experience than his older female partner. The reasons for this twist of thinking lie in the fact that younger generations are having much more sex at an earlier age and with a great many more partners.

Mature women who've been in long-standing marriages may have only had on a hand full of lovers before their husband. Their younger mate has been the beneficiary of a generation with openly sexual freedom. Here's where the tables turn. It's the younger man who can teach his older partner a thing or two; adding spice, inhibition and adventure to their sex life.

Communication skills in a relationship? How do you resolve differences?

Communication is key to establishing and maintaining a vibrant relationship. Honesty countered with sensitivity is the correct format for all information that needs to be shared. Whether you want to improve an existing situation or secure conflict resolution, communication needs to be neutral in tone in order to be "heard." Accusatory statements that begin with a "You" are bound to create defensiveness. The preferred method of sharing one's feelings is to begin with an "I" statement.

For resolving differences, I use what I call the "table approach." I discovered this approach when trying to deal with a controlling boyfriend many years ago. I needed him to understand what I was saying without feeling bad or wrong in the process. It's since proven to be an effective tool I still use today. It allows both parties to put their minds together to solve and existing problem.

I begin by putting the issue "on the table." I state what I see happening and then ask him what he thinks we can do about it. This enables him to become a part of the solution, rather than being the problem. With our joined perspective, I can see how he views his position while stating my feelings about it. Our discussion becomes neutral as we both look for possible remedies to the issue at hand.

No one is made to feel bad, wrong or defective. And, both us feel empowered.

How do you know when the relationship is over? How do you end it and remain friendly?

The only way to determine if there is life left in the relationship is if both partners desire to "try." This can be done via couples counseling, behavioral changes and honest communication. If that's done in earnest, there may be hope to create a new format for growth.

The relationship's over when there's nothing left to learn. Both partners are bored; they can far too easily predict the next sentence their mate will say and the next thing their partner will do. Stasis becomes the norm. There's no ongoing growth. Worse yet, there's no desire for ongoing growth. The relationship has clearly run its course.

Maintaining a friendship is possible after some time has past and each has stabilized as an "individual." Having been a couple is an identity, of sorts. It takes time to reclaim our own lives separate and apart from our "other."

We thank Susan for sharing such wonderful information to consider when making your Ideal Target Market list.

NEIL: I recently saw an online profile by a woman who was a former model; she had indicated a 3,000-mile radius as a "doable" geographic range to meet her match. Really? We get that long-distance romances can happen; however, would you want to begin a relationship with someone who lives on the other side of the country?

Think realistically about what a logical distance would be to travel in order to build a bond that can occur only through time spent together. We love SKYPE, Face Time and other social networking sites to stay connected, however, a long-distance relationship may have far more obstacles and hoops to jump through than most.

Here's another thought to ponder. We're fans of "niche" marketing - meaning a specific or narrow market segment. Why? We both know it's an easier marketing and sales process when you take care to be specific about what you want and how far you want to travel for love. Both of us have specific niche markets we "target" in our business, and although geography need not apply to our business models, it certainly does in our personal dating life. What "niche" are you looking for?

Remember, ladies and gentleman, this is about new partner (not business) acquisition. We are seeking a specific group of people who have similar interests, traits, characteristics, and physical qualities that we are attracted to and want more of. That's an ideal target market.

We've got to segment the market by geography, demographics, psychographics (belief systems), and "buyer" preference. Once you've determined your concentrated strategy for looking for a partner, know your niche - then you can more clearly identify the "marketing mix" you need to reach them.

We are firm believers in the AIDA formula of attracting Attention, Interest and Desire in our target market and putting our plan into Action (AIDA = Attention, Interest, Desire and Action).

Creating your wish list of ideal features and characteristics of your mate allows you to focus in on the people you want to attract- and therefore, increases the chances of you meeting this person ten-fold. Maintain a concentrated strategy of identifying your niche target market and get ready to employ a marketing mix of communication strategies to reach your market.

Sorry, we went off on a marketing and sales lingo sideline. In other words, keep focused on who you want to attract, in the geographic area you want to meet someone, and identify the number of ways you might increase your chances of meeting that special someone. Make sense? We hope so.

Honestly, it's the process of "qualifying" your target market by being open, clear and honest about what you're looking for - especially online - when you have the opportunity to share your likes and desires on a profile people are able to view prior to meeting you.

Know exactly what you are looking for in your next relationship. The Rolling Stones may say that "you can't always get what you want," but don't embrace that line when it comes to finding that person of your dreams. You can and should be very selective and specific these days. This is our opinion of course, but don't you agree?

Assuming you're at a point in your life at which you've had a few relationships and dates over the years, it's time to reflect: What did you enjoy about each of them and what were the big turn-offs?

Do you want to be with someone shy and apprehensive, or outgoing and enthusiastic? Do you prefer a person who is energetic or more laid back? Do you want someone who's active and enjoys working out and staying fit, or do you prefer a couch potato that would rather drink beer in bed while eating pretzels and watching sports with you? Do you want someone affectionate or cold and aloof? What about height, weight, build, skin and hair color?

We all get turned-on by something, so know what turns you on and what turns you off. Are you looking for a serious full-time relationship that can lead to marriage, or do you want someone to date on weekends? Do you want someone who jumps out of bed early in the morning or someone that sleeps in until noon on weekends? What about their income level and level of education?

The above are just a handful of the factors that make someone appealing to you. Then of course, we can only hope that they find you just as appealing. Be honest with yourself and you will increase your odds for a happy relationship.

NEIL: I created a list of the characteristics I was looking for when I set out to find the woman of my dreams, and I share it here as an example:
- Outgoing and positive minded
- Healthy and physically fit
- Intelligent and enjoys good conversation
- Kind to others
- Must be comfortable with affection, intimacy and lots of sex
- Likes to exercise daily: running, yoga, walking, bicycling, etc….

- Confident in herself and her abilities
- Loves to travel, go out to dinner and meet new people
- Comfortable in social settings
- Baggage-free ~ no leftovers from past relationships
- Attractive ~ at least to me!
- Financially secure
- Solid relationships with friends and family
- Independent and not "needy and clingy"

We all know that if you asked a dozen people what they would have on their list of ideal partner characteristics, it could be quite different from mine. Although we are similar in many ways, we are also very different. Wow, that's breaking news isn't it? Create your own list of the features and characteristics that YOU prefer in a man or woman.

Interests vary of course, which is why it's so important to know the type of people you want to meet. Yes, target and niche marketing is precisely what you are doing in this exercise. Know what you are looking for in the "ideal" match. They may not be perfect, since perfection doesn't really exist, but if you know what you prefer, then the results generated in your on line search will be closer to your ideal match.

Again, at this point in your life, you should know exactly what you find appealing, attractive, enticing and what WOWS you. You should also know what your deal-breakers are and what behaviors are unacceptable. Know exactly what you want and precisely what you want to avoid.

Life is too short to settle for less than your near-perfect mate! If you want proof of that, just look around at the couples that lack that spark because they've drifted apart over the years for a number of reasons. They may have more differences than similarities or perhaps they were a mismatch to begin with. Some people say that opposites attract. Magnets do, but we don't agree with that at all when it comes to great relationships. Don't let that happen to you.

It's wonderful to be with someone who adds smiles to your lips everyday! We tend to be happier when we are with people with whom we have plenty in common with. It adds more smiles to our life.

Finally, we'd like to share some tips from expert **Susan Ortolano, M.A., PCC, CMRC.** She offers 10 points to consider when trying to decide if he is "the one":

Is This the One?

10 "Musts" to consider to help you uncover that answer

Ahhh, you've been single and seeking, looking for the love of your life and met this amazing person. You've gone on some mind-blowing dates, you finish each other's sentences, you even both love just going to the grocery store and hanging out together. The chemistry is off the charts and you have never felt anything like this before. Could this amazing creature be the one? Are you sure? Are you ready?

I'm Susan Ortolano, and as an Intuitive Relationship Coach and Educator, I work with singles who are having these exact experiences and are asking themselves these very questions, and many more.

So, how do you know if you have met your ideal partner, the one you have waited your whole life for? How do you know if you are as prepared as you think you are to find and be with "the One"?

Let's look at some tips that might help.

Here are my 10 'musts' to consider as you prepare for and evaluate so you can answer those questions for yourself.

1) If you are dating, wait it out - There are several stages of a relationship. The Courtship Stage is the first one. Getting past that to the next stages will help you better evaluate if this is truly the One. So, wait it out a bit longer. Chemistry is an essential component, and is very present during the Courtship Stage, but never underestimate the power of compatibility, shared interests, and overall alignment. The Courtship Stage, while beautiful and amazing, doesn't necessarily indicate that this person is the one, and has you so high in the clouds you may almost forget your name. Let yourself come down a bit and get to know the person before making a decision.

2) Know what you are looking for - It surprised me as I started coaching singles, how many of them didn't have deep clarity about what they wanted in a partner. It is easy to state the things that are on the surface, such as appearance, financial stability, good health, a nice car, along with some of the other material things desired in a partner and in a relationship, but many people forget to list some of the deeper, more important qualities they are looking for that will make or break a relationship. Having a 'cute butt' can be on your list, but that butt will droop at some point, so make sure there are other qualities that can warm your heart for a lifetime.

3) Identify and release your 'stories' - We all have 'sto-

ries' or beliefs about how the world works, who we are, what relationship is supposed to look like, how men are, how women are and they are all based on our history. What we have experienced in the past often influences who we attract and how we operate in a relationship. In my programs for singles, as well as for couples, working on releasing the 'Once upon a time in a land where things were so bad' stories we carry is critical and, to find the right partner, releasing the stories can help evaluate more authentically. When you heal your history, your ideal partner will be much easier to recognize. Plus, you will find someone who aligns with the authentic you vs. the 'you' of stories past.

4) Live your life - Many singles are so focused on finding the right partner that they forget to nurture and develop the other areas of their life. The best thing to do is to have the rest of your life be successful and amazing, while still allowing yourself to be open to meeting people and evaluating the people you are dating. Living a great life keeps you interested and interesting. I know it is difficult to be alone, but alone and lonely don't have to be the same thing. Whether you are still searching or currently dating, make your life awesome!

5) Choose the right venues - Online dating, while convenient, may not always be the right venue for meeting the right person. I know it is frustrating to figure out where to go to meet someone. Attending events, activities, and pursuing your own interests are the best ways to meet people because you will have more in common with them besides just 'Hey, we're both single!' While there may be some chemistry, you

may not likely have enough shared interests in common or some of the other qualities you are seeking. If you have met someone at a singles event, notice if you have enough in common.

6) Know your deal-breakers - One of the most important things that can help you determine if someone is the one is to know the qualities and behaviors that would have someone NOT be the one. It is hard to notice 'red flags' at the beginning because it is easy to get so caught up in the hot chemistry, but when you know what your deal-breakers are, the things that someone would say, do, want, or be that would have you run for the hills, you will recognize them more quickly and not waste your time on someone who isn't right for you.

7) Connect with yourself - Grow, evolve, read books, attend events that help you continue to develop yourself personally. The more healing and growing you do as a single, the less you need to heal when you find your partner. Growing still happens when you are partnered, but take care of the heavy stuff now, and you will be more attuned to who your right partner is while you are dating. It is much easier to determine if this amazing creature is the right one for you when you are deeply connected with yourself.

8) Be choosy - You deserve to have the great love of your life. Create a personal vision of your ideal partner and don't ever settle for less. Know your own boundaries and guidelines for dating and sexual interaction, and if someone you are dating doesn't respect your guidelines, show them the door because they aren't the one for you.

9) Be aware - When evaluating whether someone is right for you, be aware of how you are being treated, how they are treating themselves and others, how they are with your friends. Be aware of how often they want to interact with you, their core values, their desire to have a relationship, and be aware of how these things align with you. Acute awareness can keep you honest with yourself.

10) Hire a qualified Relationship Coach - You don't have to figure this out alone. A good Relationship Coach can help guide you through the process, help you discover things about yourself you hadn't known, remembered, or realized in years, can help you identify your core values, your strengths, your relationship deal-breakers and vision, as well as remind you of your sense of value to help you prepare for, clarify, and find the great love of your life.

While these will be helpful in determining who is the right partner for you, there is so much more to explore. Working with a qualified Relationship Coach can help take you to that special moment you've waited for, when you `know you've met 'The One.'

Chapter 4

Plant Your Seeds Where You Want them to Grow Using a "Media Mix" to Find True Love

Once you know your ideal target market, the next step is to think about where you can be "canvassing" for love in all the right places.

There's a saying among marketers that "you're only as good as your list" - that is your database of prospects, clients, referral sources, etc. We believe the same is true when looking for love. You've got to create a network of referral sources for you to get to know other people in your situation: single and looking for love or a connection with someone.

Right about now, you may be thinking, "Wait a minute— What's this talk about referral? I thought this book was all about using the Internet." The answer is, while we do devote much attention in this book to online search, that is by no means the only avenue we suggest you take to pursue your goal.

We know how tough a challenge it is to get out there and "get back on the horse" so to speak, after being suddenly single at mid-life. It may feel like a mountain to climb. That was certainly how each of us reacted when, after long-term marriages - we felt like awkward pubescent kids - we were left looking for love in all the wrong places (or not looking at all).

It did give us more empathy for our kids, who were experiencing the same weirdness that we were, but the timing was not what we were hoping for and seemed "way off."

We also found out that people will not seek you out by knocking on your door to announce that they heard you were available and would like to go out. Not happening.

So what's a man or woman to do? Here's one idea we DON'T recommend in business - and we certainly wouldn't recommend it when seeking out love: No cold calling allowed. Every significant business deal that we've made has been the result of a "warm" call or referral.

We are dating in exciting times today. As we indicated earlier, although we are enthusiastic supporters of online search, we are also believers that there are many other ways to "get the word out" and generate some word of mouth marketing that might eventually lead you to that wonderful guy or girl you've been waiting to meet.

NANCY: In almost every seminar I give that's related to marketing, I use what I call "VCR" - I know, it's embarrassing how I date myself! VCR stands for Visibility, Consistency and Repetition in the marketplace. You need to be visible in a consistent way and repeat that message and image over time.

Other marketers call it "Reach and Frequency." Who are you reaching out to and how frequently? There's an advertising rule of thumb that it takes at least six impressions before someone recognizes you or your product or service before they make the connection of who you are and what you're attempting to sell.

As long as we're into acronyms, let's not forget to mention that we're firm believers in the AIDA formula of attracting Attention, Interest and Desire in our target market and putting our plan into Action (AIDA = Attention, Interest, Desire and Action).

To review: First, you create your wish list of ideal features and characteristics of your mate which will allow you to focus in on the people you want to attract- and thereby, increase the chances of your eventually meeting this person ten-fold. Second, you maintain a concentrated strategy of identifying your niche target market and get ready to employ a marketing mix of communication strategies to reach your market.

Sorry, we just went off on a marketing and sales lingo sideline. In other words, keep focused on who you want to attract, in the geographic area you want to meet someone, and identify the number of ways you might increase your chances of meeting that special someone. Make sense? We hope so.

Business Expert Stacey Alcorn breaks it all down for us into easy-to-follow steps. Here's her advice:

What's your strategic dating plan? That's right, you should totally have a business plan when it comes to dating. If you were building your own Fortune 500 Company, which perhaps you are working on, you work off a plan, right? Shouldn't you put as much, or even more effort into creating a success strategy for finding the person you are going to spend the rest of your life with? Since you're already familiar with what a business plan looks like, here's how it would compare to a strategic dating plan:

1. Vision/Mission Statement - Your business plan always includes your vision for the future and your mission, which describes how you plan on getting there. For example, with my real estate offices, it's something like this. "We will be the number one real estate offices in New England based on transactions closed and per agent productivity. We will achieve this by aligning ourselves as partners in every community we do business in. We will be the go-to resource for information about our towns and we will be the company that each community seeks out when someone's in need." Short and sweet, but it makes a declaration of what our goal is and how we generally plan on doing it.

What's your dating mission statement? Here's an example: "I will meet a spouse who is loving, caring, and supportive of my hectic work schedule. He is someone that loves kids, volunteers in the community, and has his own hobbies and friends as well. I will find him by spending time in the places where he spends time, like church, community groups, or civic organizations."

2. Prospecting - In a business plan it is essential to lay out a timeline for hitting prospecting goals. How many potential clients and what kind of clients must be touched each day, week, and year? Your strategic dating plan is much the same. There have been countless examples offered throughout the book as to where to find a potential date, so this is where you list the ones you will focus on and create a system for regularly and consistently prospecting for your mate. As you are prospecting, keep track of your wins. For example if there's one method that often brings you more successful dates, stick to that stream instead of moving to another.

3. Goals - In business, I love goal setting because it's important to have something to shoot for. If you have fuzzy business goals, you get fuzzy business results. The same is true in dating. If you have a fuzzy dating goal, like "I hope to someday find love," you will get fuzzy dating results, like maybe someday in the next fifty years you will find a suitable match. If however, you are clear and specific in your goals, it's easy to determine if you are on target or falling short. For example, "I will meet one new single person for coffee once a week. I will find him/her from online sites, my volunteer groups, work, and outings that I attend. I will find my new mate by the end of the year." This is much more specific and easier to track. If one week goes by with no coffee date, you are falling short of your goal and it's time to readjust the sails of your ship.

Create a strategic dating plan today and watch as you start to see concrete results. Be precise, systematized, and consistent, and favorable results will follow.

If this all seems incredibly unromantic and highly calculated - we know. There is some truth to this concept, though. We also have faith and believe that there can be love at first sight and if that's what has happened to you - we love those stories.

Here are some ideas to get you started in your "lead -generation" strategy. That's right, you are generating leads for persons of interest in meeting someone amazing - like you - by actively pursuing your ideal target market. As you develop your list, remember to *fish where the fish are*. How can the mate of your dreams find you if you're not visible in places where other singles are likely to be? The odds would be against you.

• Check out online dating sites. Ask your friends what ones they've been on that have worked for them in introducing them to nice people. Commit to sending at least three messages a day to people you find interesting.

• What clubs or community events or activities could you participate in to meet people who are like-minded?

• Let your friends and family members know you'd like to meet someone. Everyone knows someone who's single and might want to meet someone they know, like and trust.

• NANCY: My mom and dad met on a blind date and have been happily married for 50+ years now. Just sayin'— if it hadn't been for a blind date, I wouldn't be here right now.

• Get physical and get outside! Take a walk and start to talk to people.

• Take a class through your local Adult Education Center, college, museum, or store.

• Get out there and do something new. Sign up for a ski weekend for singles, take a trip with a friend, and go on a singles cruise. The key is to mix it up in order to find your ideal "target" love interest.

• Change your routine - take a different route to work, try a new restaurant, make a new dish, visit a town you'd like to see and haven't been to, read a new book. The key is to do something different that might open your eyes to new and fun possibilities with or without a special someone.

Speaking of *fishing where the fish are*, as we were a moment ago, **Stacey Alcorn** notes that:

If you're looking for fish, a good place to start is in

the ocean—and in the dating world, that means, what else? Facebook!

Facebook is an important tool both in business and dating because it offers us a bird's eye view into the life of someone we want to get to know better. Even without formally friend-requesting someone, most Facebook profiles are set up so that the public may view them, which means you can check out someone even before going on a date. Do they like kids? Are they positive and upbeat? Do they drink too much? Did they recently go through a difficult break up?

Forget checking an online dating profile for photos of someone; check Facebook instead for the real deal. Facebook often tells all. It is your resume both for business and in life. As a business owner, I always check a potential employee's social media sites to see what type of person she's hiring. I believe the same should be done when dating.

Don't forget, social media is a two way street. What are potential candidates going to see about you? In 2013, I had a friend that had gone through a very difficult breakup. For months, every post she put on Facebook was negative, and she often made personal attacks on the guy she'd been dating. One day I picked up the phone and asked her, "When the next perfect companion comes along and checks out your Facebook page, do you think he's going to want to date you?"

What she didn't realize, before I got her attention, was that the negative status updates weren't hurting her ex, they were hurting her. She was documenting her pessimism and anger for the world to see, and sooner or later those posts would drive away her knight in shining armor. After our conversation she started cleaning up her posts, and before long she found Mr. Right, and yes, she found him on Facebook.

Chapter 5

Create an Online Profile That Will Generate Results

Marketing and sales are two areas of expertise for us because we've been involved and very successful in both for dozens of years. When you create your profile on Match, Facebook or Linked-in, you are actually marketing yourself to a potential partner. Your profile should be designed to quickly catch the attention of the people "shopping" or browsing around.

Think of your profile as an advertisement or a commercial on television. In business, this is known as your "one sheet." It describes you, shows your physical attributes (in the form of a photo), and gives viewers an overview of who you are and what you like. It offers a quick impression to someone who is using the Web as part of their search for their perfect match.

When people look at your profile, they'll often decide within seconds if they want to learn more about you or if they should scroll on to the next profile. We know that sounds cold as ice, but it is reality, and sometimes the truth hurts. Consider us the friends who will give it to you straight up and not sugarcoat our advice. That's why you're reading this book, right?

Advertisers know that they have about two seconds to grab your attention. Some companies are extremely competent at it, while others fail. They spend millions of dollars to find out what colors, captions, and designs capture your eyes and emotions.

Andy Warhol was great at capturing "pop culture" and making it into memorable artwork - really "borrowing" what was already created and putting his spin on it. *So, why re-create the wheel here?*

Think about a stroll through a supermarket - there are dozens of cans of corn, but one appeals to you more than the others. Why? For some reason, and it is not by accident, it just jumps out at you.

Marketers intentionally design products to stand out from the crowd and grab your attention. So, why would it be any different when people are looking at your profile and photos?

Obviously, some will find you attractive and appealing while others will not. No big deal. You'll feel the same way about the profiles and photos you review.

NEXT! The point we're making here is, as we say in sales and marketing, you can't take rejection personally. If you do, it is an overwhelming possibility that this unwarranted sensitivity could put a major damper on your dating life. If someone doesn't respond to you, you've just got to remind yourself that it's not personal, because they haven't had the pleasure of knowing you yet. Simply move on to the next bachelor or bachelorette.

We repeat, you only have a couple seconds to get someone's attention, so keep that in mind when you create your profile and, certainly, when you show up for a date. We want you to grab the attention of those individuals in your target market, so that you get more of an opportunity to present yourself. We want you to be successful in this marketing campaign and what you write in the profile can seal the deal!

So, getting down to the nitty-gritty: **What makes a good profile?** There are so many factors that combine to help your profile stand out among the other millions. The photos, what and how you write about yourself, your grammar, specific details of what you're looking for in your ideal match, and how you describe yourself will all contribute to how your profile is perceived by potential partners. Spelling correctly is always a bonus, but you might be mildly surprised at the numerous typos we've seen.

Take your time creating your profile because it is the engine of your dating future. Be creative and have fun with it. If you have a mental block, some companies, such as Match.com, will create a profile for you at a nominal cost. Many people ask a friend or two to create a profile for them, so you have a few options to consider.

When you're drafting your profile, write as if you are having a conversation with someone who has asked you to describe yourself. If we were out for lunch with you, and casually asked about your life, and the things you like to do that make you happy, what would you say?

It's our guess that we'd have quite an interesting conversation and we'd learn so much about you. Write your profile as if we were having a chat while we sip a favorite beverage. What are you passionate about in your life? What do you do when you aren't at work? Where do you enjoy going on vacation and what do you like to do when you get there?

Each of us has read thousands of profiles during our search for our near-perfect match. Unfortunately, many of these profiles are pitiful and terribly boring. We don't believe those people *are* actually boring - it's just that they simply don't know what to write or how to "market" themselves. This book will assist you in finding the match of your dreams or, at least, help you find someone fun to date, build a relationship with and share some happiness.

Examples of Women's Profiles:

1. I like a man with a good sense of humor, since I love to laugh and would love someone to laugh with. A dry sense of humor is really appealing to me. I value a man who is able to balance work and play. Someone who enjoys life and being with people is important to me, as well as a man who is active and energetic. If you are curious and passionate about life, that's a plus. I am drawn to people who pay it forward.

I'm in a good place in my life. Life is pretty amazing. I am open to love and being loved. I work hard and play hard but appreciate quiet moments in between. I love meeting people and enjoy being with my family and friends. Love being outdoors. I like to dance (all kinds), and know how to sail, ski and bike ride and while I don't love the gym I go. Yes I like to put on a little black dress and go out on the town now and then. I make an effort each day to appreciate the moment. I love learning from others and trying new things. I value the simpler things in life but like anyone else can enjoy the finer things as well. I can mix with anyone. I like to read, visit museums, and go to shows. I love to cheer for the Sox and Pats. Congrats Sox on the World Series! Go Pats!

2. I'm a happy person, who loves her job, enjoys knowing that I made a difference in someone's day, or even life sometimes. Making someone else feel good is one of my greatest pleasures. I will take a chance and try anything once. I love the outdoors, the beaches, and warm weather. I love traveling, and would love to do more of it. My hobbies consist of remodeling, tearing anything apart I can get my hands on, from flooring to refinishing furniture, love gardening, and I'm pretty handy in most construction. Creativity is my specialty.

3. I feel very grateful for all the blessings in my life. I have a very full life with family and friends but I am looking for that one special someone to include in my world. I am an active, healthy, and outgoing person who loves exploring new places and creating new adventures! My ideal man would have a fulfilling life in terms of work, family and friends, and would want to include me in that part of his life as well. I am looking for someone who will let me be me. I can be silly and playful and full of energy! Open mindedness, a sense of humor, and the ability to keep his word are the traits most valued. Generosity, chivalry and willingness to learn and explore new things always make me smile! I want someone who values a healthy lifestyle in terms of exercise and eating, but enjoys letting loose and letting his hair down, as well! I am looking for a special man who will have a passion for expanding their horizons and willingness to travel and see the world....there is so much to see and experience and time passes so quickly!! I am both food and fashion flexible. I love to cook, and enjoy making eclectic meals for my friends and family; yet simply adore it when someone offers to cook for me. Enjoy dressing up in a skirt and

heels, as well as dressing down in jeans. While I aim to be low-maintenance, I never leave home without my lipstick and my cell phone. With these two items in hand, I'm good to go just about anywhere.

Each of these profiles gives us some insight to the women who wrote them. Cooking, traveling, remodeling, gardening, low-maintenance, the beaches and the outdoors, their attitude and what type of guy they enjoy the most. They also give an interested party plenty to respond to. When a guy responds to any of these women, he can, and should, mention what he liked about what he read and if he shares their interests.

Some profiles are five times longer than these examples. So, what length of a profile is ideal? We like the longer version because it tells us so much more about the person we are interested in. If you feel comfortable writing five paragraphs about you, your interests, turn-ons and turn-offs, then please go ahead. This isn't a one-minute commercial at the Super Bowl. Write all you like and cast a wide net to your target market.

Creating a profile is the most important first step you should accomplish. It provides the reader with some insight about you, your hobbies, attitude, interests and the type of person you want to date. It should let people know what you are passionate about, what type of personality you have and what you enjoy doing when you aren't working.

Don't leave people guessing who you are or what your personality is like, or else you won't receive many emails with an expressed interest. The goal of being on dating sites is to find someone to date and, perhaps, build a solid relationship with. Well, that begins with knowing exactly what you are looking for in a person and knowing what you have to offer someone.

After you know exactly what you are looking for in a person, make sure to lay it out in your profile. The options and preferences cover just about everything…height, build, age, education, career interests, favorite travel locations, income range, with kids or no kids, favorite sports and activities, things to do on dates, books, food, etc. If your profile specifically lists all of these details, then the likelihood of finding your match is much greater.

Of course, personality and other interests are critically important. Agreeing to a date only because someone is attractive or because his or her stated income is $150,000+, is likely to be a disappointment, in our opinion. Nevertheless, what each of us was looking for when we were searching may be completely different from what YOU are looking for.

NANCY: A good buddy of Neil's has been on four dates with different women and each one spent the night with him in a hotel, on the first date. Why am I not surprised? Sure, sex and intimacy are nothing to be ashamed of; however, it's just my opinion that "hooking up" from a dating site may not be the best "foundation" for building a relationship. If someone has had four dates with different women, each of whom spent the night with him in a hotel, I consider that a potential health risk, and not a great start to an intimate connection to boot-hookup or no.

Nevertheless, the point we want to get across is: we can all find what we are looking for on these sites.
We assume you want that "spark" - that chemistry of a

great fit - and plenty in common with someone. We know it's not easy, but people really do meet their ideal matches every day. Just be honest with yourself about the characteristics you are looking for. Then again, some of the profiles state clearly that they do not want a serious relationship but, instead, want to "hook up" and have fun. We repeat - know what you are looking for and you will most likely find it.

NEIL: Be specific on your profile page and not vague. This quote sums it up: "If you don't know where you are going, then any road will take you there." Some of the profiles, in fact many profiles, are too nondescript and wishy-washy. For example, here's one where the preferred height is listed as between 3 - 7 feet!

NANCY: OK, part of me laughs out loud when I see someone who has a sense of humor (however, not if *all* responses are silly or meant to be funny), but as far as height and age range - I'm more open to a "wide" range.

Alternatively, we've seen profiles that state "Not sure" on the topic of kids. Some people are trying to leave a door open to fit into someone else's world. Many use the phrase "I'll tell you later" for some of their preferences. When you go shopping for your dream home or ideal car, you likely know what you want, what wows you, what turns you off and what is going to make you smile every time you step in the door. Finding that special person in your life is difficult enough, so don't be vague and don't settle for just anyone. Time is precious and we encourage you not to spend or waste time on "maybes" in life.

Dating Success After 40

Our experience in online dating search sites is primarily with Match.com because each of us found it easier to maneuver around and search for those people we are attracted to. The eHarmony company runs their business a bit differently. While Match will send an email with a dozen Daily Matches, eHarmony will send possible date matches to you throughout the day. Their profiling system is one of the best in the business because it's so much more comprehensive. However, don't be shocked to receive profiles from people more than 1,000 miles away. You cannot create searches for profiles on eHarmony like you can on Match.com.

We've shared a few female profiles, so we would be remiss not to also share a few of the men's. Some of these profiles are terrific, while others are quite frightening! A profile should give the reader an idea of your personality. Instead of writing that you are funny, why not share your humorous side in the profile? We consider this first example to be one of the better profiles. It's from a guy in Washington who lets his personality shine through.

Examples of Men's Profiles:

1. Congratulations! You have just landed on what could possibly be the last profile that you will ever have to read. Well…there is sometimes a fine line between "putting your best foot forward" and sounding like a jerk, but I'll do the best that I can. Let' s see…If I had any friends they would describe me as intelligent, thoughtful, witty and romantic. I do my best to show that chivalry is not dead yet (maybe just on life support)! I'm loyal as a dog and I greatly value family and friends. In fact, I come from a large close knit family, and I'm happy to report there are very few brawls at family gatherings :-) I enjoy playing guitar, practicing martial arts, traveling and cookouts on the deck. I am fortunate to own a beautiful home (very romantic I'm told) and enjoy doing the home improvement projects that make it even nicer. As if that's not enough, I've also never been convicted of anything and I can order a beer in four languages. I enjoy great physical, emotional and financial health. I have been blessed in life. My philosophy: work hard, play hard, take a few chances along the way, and you should have few regrets when you get to that "long blink" at the end.

Do you see why we think this profile is one of the best we've ever read? His personality is evident in his writing. He's funny, interesting, balanced in life, and at first glance he's very open to sharing who he is and what he does for fun.

Here's another profile that you might enjoy.

2. I would like to meet a fit, outgoing, energetic optimist who enjoys traveling, dining at restaurants, homemade meals (I love to cook), LIFE and being with enthusiastic friends! I enjoy new adventures and went skydiving over Newport in August. Also enjoyed a great day of white-water rafting in Oregon last week. Driving a racecar at 154 mph was also a "Blast" and so was walking over blazing hot coals. Next on the Bucket List is scuba diving or anything else that I believe will WOW us! We only live once they say, so I'm going for it, doing all I can and living life to the fullest! Join me?

I am a very positive person ~ everyday! My friends would describe me as kind, generous, considerate, friendly, active, positive and very fit. I've learned to "go with the flow" in most situations that would "rattle" other people. My experiences as a professional speaker and busy traveler have taught me that lesson! Somehow, most things in life happen for a reason and eventually work out for the best! So enjoy the moment and be kind! I am a true believer in paying it forward ~ always have been and will do so forever! I also love to laugh, have fun, entertain and cook for friends at my home.

This second profile tells us exactly what type of woman he wants to meet. Some women may say he's shallow because he's only looking for someone fit - but give him credit. He knows what he wants and is very specific about it. You can also see, clearly, what his personality is. That's the type of profile we encourage you to write. Tell everyone who you are, what you are looking for in a match and what you love to do.

Hopefully, you've seen enough profiles to give you more ideas on creating or improving your own. Expect to change your profile on occasion and add new photos from your recent experiences. Have fun with the creative side of your brain when you are designing, or redesigning, your profile. As we mentioned before, searching for potential dates is something like fishing. You have to know where to fish, which bait to use to catch exactly what you want, and you must be patient, as well as persistent.

A Picture is Worth a Thousand Words

This is your big opportunity to catch someone's eye and interest, so put plenty of effort into selecting the photos you use in your profile, a.k.a. your marketing campaign. Think of your photo as your headshot in your business "Press Kit."

Let's face it, we all have a certain "look" we desire that makes our heart beat a bit faster than normal. There is a "WOW" factor that catches our eye. Then, hopefully, the chemistry during the first phone call or date creates more interest or, perhaps, catches our heart.

However, the little fire in our heart often starts with a physical attraction to the other person you have an interest in. Therefore, post the best photos you have, or have new photos taken. While you may opt for a professional photographer who can portray you in the best way possible using modern technology, we don't believe you need to invest hundreds of dollars for photos. A good friend can also take photos of you, but that's your choice, of course. Marketing companies talk about "truth in advertising," but when it comes to online dating, some people are less than honest. Some are actually fraudulent. They lie about their height, weight and yes, even the way they look. *Caveat emptor*, or, let the buyer beware!

Your photos should be current. Let us explain what we mean by "current" - like within the last 12 months, not 15 years ago! Yes - you heard us correctly. Current doesn't mean the college yearbook photo from 1980 (should you be so lucky to have graduated then)! There's no bigger turn off than seeing someone in person who has clearly sent in a photo taken 20 years ago. It may woo someone to make a connection, but trust us, if you're not up front from the beginning, it won't last. Guys are especially guilty of this.

NEIL: Both of us have been shocked several times when we showed up for a first date and the person looked nothing like their photo on the profile. Just last week, one of my female friends met a guy for lunch. She liked his profile and his photos, and was intrigued that he was a marathon runner. Now get this: He showed up to lunch with a potbelly, weighing about 250 pounds, and it was obvious that if he ran marathons, it was many years and many pounds ago. So, she asked him on the spot when he ran his last marathon. It was 25 years ago.

NANCY: I know a man who lied in his profile and said he was a "widower." He met a woman he was attracted to and continued with this lame and untrue story. Guess what? He liked her so much that when she shared with him the fact that she hadn't met someone she wanted to be serious with because they were all liars - he 'fessed up. That was their last date, despite the good time that was had by all. His lying was a deal breaker. She was not going there. Period. So, he was left to go "fishing" again. Too bad!

During our research for this book, we spoke with dozens of people to gain insight into their online dating experiences. Far too many told us that the guys and gals often had photos in their profile that were more than a dozen years old and taken when they were in shape, had hair, didn't have a massive potbelly and when they were exercising consistently. Therefore, of course, their first impression when they finally met was about the person's credibility and trustworthiness. If they already misrepresented themselves before the first date, what else are they going to lie about? That's not a good start to a relationship!

One of the BIG lessons we learned about photos is simple, and we recommend you pay close attention to this one. If the person you are interested in ONLY has one photo in their profile and they look amazingly young for a 45 year-old, then the photo is probably not a current photo. It's true there are some men and women who have a more youthful look today than ever before, but you may want to make a respectful request to see "more." If they come through, you'll know they're willing to show their "current" self - the one you'd be dating. If not, they will "fade away" like the lack of photographic images they're willing (or unwilling) to provide.

Don't lie or deceive in your profile. If you lie about who you are, what you look like or what you do, when the truth comes out it hurts everyone. You will be doomed for failure. Please use current photos. Thank you!

We encourage you to share 5-10 photos. One isn't enough and fifteen might be overkill, but if they are great photos then go for it! It seems like the most confident people share up to 25 photos. Why not? Be sure to include a side view, front view and maybe even a rear view if you like. We all have a different body type that we like, so you'll appeal to someone.

Please don't add photos of previous lovers or ex-spouses. We're also not fans of "cutting" them out of photos either. It's not appealing and it looks like you still have feelings for them. Nobody wants to start a relationship with someone that is still holding onto an old lover. We want to know that you are over your old love and ready to start this new chapter fresh, with a clean slate. You can relay this by using photos that show you in the best light, with a smile and a happy facial expression.

Granted, not everyone is by nature happy and enthusiastic. If you tend to be miserable, pessimistic, rarely smile, and are grumpy most of the time, then share those photos, also. Not everyone wants to be with a happy person. Negative people should surround themselves with other negative people, so they can talk about gloom and doom. No, we aren't trying to be funny. The same idea works for happy people: surround yourself with other optimists who love life, people and each day. The goal here is to find someone you are compatible with, in most key areas of your life.

The photos should be of YOU! We've seen far too many profiles with photos of mountains, dogs, sunsets, beaches, horses and cats. I'm not dating the dog, cat or horse or even your car. We are interested in the person that the profile is written about. A few photographers like to add their favorite sunset photo. For example, it's perfectly reasonable to have one sunset photo in your collection if it's there because it shows the great view from your deck on the bay.

NEIL: When preparing to take your photos, dress up, look fantastic and present yourself as if you were going to a holiday dinner, out to a club, off to the gym, or for a walk on the beach. Wear the outfit(s) that you feel most confident in. I remember the television commercials in the 1970s that encouraged guys to "Look sharp! Feel sharp!" The commercials were for a razor blade company and were very effective in getting our attention. Another effective advertisement is that of Men's Warehouse that states, "You're gonna like the way you look. I guarantee it!"
Select appropriate outfits to express the different sides of your personality. Share photos of how you look in jeans, shorts, eveningwear, yoga clothes, or even a bathing suit (if

you are comfortable). Be careful not to overdo any particular type of clothing - variety is the key. Oftentimes, showing only one facet of yourself can be a set up to attract what you might not want 24/7.

Realize that what you wear in your photo will attract someone to your profile, so be aware of the on the message you are sending. Guys, please keep your shirt on unless you're at the beach - and don't even think of sending a "selfie" from the bathroom mirror. Another photo to avoid is the one with you holding the fish you caught. It's overdone, and the ladies say it looks stupid. The same applies to the photos of you partying your brains out with the guys at the football game. When women see that, they wonder if you'll have any time for them on the weekends during the football season.

~

NANCY: I've seen many profile pictures featuring guys in tank tops and torn shorts. Not doin' it for me If someone can't put their best foot forward in an online photo, what are the chances they can present themselves appropriately when meeting my friends or going out to dinner at someplace a step above Applebee's?

Women are guilty of the same. Some women post a photo showing themselves dressed in very suggestive clothing and doing all they could to show off the "girls' stuff" to catch the eyes of the guys. It will definitely get attention - but maybe not the kind you were actually looking for. The last things I want a man focused on are specific body parts when sitting across from me. There will be plenty of time for that later, assuming things go well and there's mutual attraction.

NEIL: Yeah, I second that. One profile of a woman had 15 photos of her in different bikinis. While she looked amazing, sexy and oh, so beautiful, I wondered what she was really marketing, so I never contacted her. Nevertheless, one would guess that many guys did!

Whatever you do, be yourself. Just know that what you wear will attract someone to your profile. Be sure you are attracting the type of people you are interested in dating.

NANCY: OK, it's quite obvious that Neil has his biases when looking for a woman to date. He will only date women who are fit, outgoing, confident, and have a touch of class. I think the "touch of class" could be upped, but that's just my opinion.

I appreciate someone who loves theatre, the arts, being social with friends and families— and ideally, someone who takes care of himself physically and emotionally. This may be a gross generalization, but I do think women are more forgiving of a few extra pounds on their man than the other way around.

OK, one final caution: don't try to take your own photo, either with a cell phone while you strain and squint to focus on looking at the lens, or in front of a mirror, (where the flash will blur you in an instant). Sadly, we've seen more of these photos than we care to. Some of the photos in these online profiles have been hilarious while others are just pitiful. Again, ask a friend to help you so that the photos look appealing and you look relaxed.

After you have taken your photos, upload them to your profile. If you are not that technically sophisticated

Nancy Michaels & Neil Wood

and don't know how to upload photos, go to your local photo store, or ask a teenager how to do it - both are great resources.

The easiest way to upload photos is simple. Save your favorite photos on your computer desktop and add a title such as Profile1, Profile2, and Profile3. Then go to your online Profile page, click on the Photos tab, and you will be given the opportunity to Upload Photos. You can only upload one at a time, but it only takes a few seconds.

When you finish adding all the photos you want and we encourage you to add at least five, click on the Finished Adding Photos button. The photos usually need approval by the website before they will actually appear in your profile. This approval process may take an hour or more, so be patient. You'll receive an email when your photos are approved.

Many of the online dating sites will also offer to post your photos for you. You need to email the photos to the website and they will take care of the rest.

According to **Ginger Burr**, of **Total Image Consultants**, your online photo should offer viewers a glimpse into your heart and soul. You want to stand out from the crowd not because you are more attractive than every other person online (beauty is subjective anyway), but because your picture captures who you are at a deep level.

Here are a few of **Burr's** tips to do just that:

- You have to love how you look in the photo. If you don't like it, keep taking them.
- Ideally, have your photograph professionally done. These are casual shots so you don't need a stiff business headshot. You want someone who can put you at ease and capture your essence.

- If your hair is fussy or you always feel better after having your hair done, have it done before you take the pictures. Keep it natural. You don't want to look like you are going to a wedding and you don't want to present an image you cannot recreate. When you go on a date, the person should recognize you easily from your picture.

- Wear your absolute best color - and that's rarely black or white! Choose a color you feel great in. When in doubt, here are four colors that look good on a lot of people: deep teal, rich periwinkle (blue/purple), watermelon or forest green. Color does a lot to make your eyes sparkle and your skin look smooth and vibrant.

- Use accessories to add sparkle, sophistication or fun. The only accessory to avoid in a photograph is sunglasses. People need to be able to see your eyes - they communicate who you are.

- Look directly into the camera as if you are connecting personally with the person you want to attract and smile! But, nothing too sexy unless you want to attract the creepy guys.

Chapter 6

Avoiding A Crisis: Security for Online Dating

Hey, Dudes and Dudettes - Safety First. We're serious here. It's a tough world out there - dating and otherwise - and we want to help. Consumer fraud runs rampant on the online dating sites; chat rooms and anyplace else you are "meeting" someone on the Internet. Don't fall for the "bait and switch" of these crooks!

Twenty years ago, online dating wasn't even a thought. Ten years ago, it was weird. Five years ago, it was new and exciting. Today, it's as normal as milk and bread—if you're looking for a mate online, you will eventually find someone. Really. Most of our friends who've tried it were successful.

But as you probably know, by the time a new technology becomes normalized, scammers, who are usually ahead of the curve, are lying in wait. And so it has been with online dating. All the while it was gradually gaining popularity and acceptance, scammers were busy, coming up with ways to take advantage and perfecting their craft. And now it's their full-time job. They know all the new scams and come up with better ways of executing the old ones. It's today's version of Pirates - online and off!

NANCY: Our friend and colleague, **Robert Siciliano**, is a security expert; you've probably seen him on a myriad of national and international television shows. His first passion has always been personal security, as indeed it was when I first met him - ah, circa 1987? (Say it isn't so!) - Security as it relates to violence prevention.

Robert has been in the security business for more than 20 years - inspired in part as a result of violence in his own life, which prompted him to write, speak and train in self-defense. The security threat is still with us today—no different than back then, with the exception that there are many more ways for the bad guys to prey on their prospective victims. So, Robert has helped us put together the very useful tips offered in this chapter.

Studies show dating and matchmaking services in general have continued to grow, even during the recession. Many single men and women are logging in and attending speed-dating sessions, online matchmaking sites and meeting people at bars or in chat rooms, more than ever before Why? People want to connect and be connected with one another - in good times and in bad. The results can be amazingly positive or catastrophically negative.

There are a couple of reasons for the increase specifically in online dating. One, it's cheaper to join a service than it is to spend all kinds of money on a dinner and a bad blind date. Second, people want the comfort of being with someone in turbulent times. Having a companion to share in the fear, uncertainty and doubt can help people vent and find relief in each other. Many simply want companionship and intimacy that might have been lacking in their past lives.

However, in our never-ending quest to Find Mr. or Mrs. Right, the one under-discussed, overlooked and "it can't happen to me" aspect of being on the dating scene is your personal security. There are several reasons why we - as humans - tend to want to look the other way, and several reasons why we shouldn't.

Be careful to:

1. Look for red flags.

If you are contacted online and the sender makes no reference to you or your name, it may be a "broadcast" scam going to several others - not just to you as an individual. If they immediately start talking about marriage and love and showing immediate affection, run, really fast. Anyone asking for money for any reason is a con man or woman - not someone who is truly interested in wanting to make a real connection with you (with, or more importantly without, your money).

Another red flag is: when communicating with someone online and it seems it takes days for them to respond, this may be a sign they are married.

NANCY: When I first got on an online dating site, I was hearing from someone whose name was Walden (after Walden Pond in my town of Concord, MA) and had no photo. Warning signs went up for me. After several email conversations, I asked for a photo and when that message wasn't acknowledged, I asked if he "knew" me. It ended abruptly. Did it mean he was in fact married? Maybe, maybe not, but either way - it was weird and not what I had anticipated on a singles dating site. Buyer beware!

2. When communicating with a potential mate via online dating or even in the physical world, please do not give up all your information to them until you are entirely sure they are "good" or "decent" people. This process can take weeks if not months - but according to Siciliano, "it's worth the wait." Bad guys lie - and often - with little to no conscience. Most will keep up the ruse until they have what they need or until you are in a vulnerable position. Please be discreet and keep your personal information private.

3. Read books on self-defense and personal security. This may seem really scary and unnatural, however, it's always best to be safe rather than sorry. Watch instructional videos on self-defense techniques and sign up for a self-defense course. The single most effective self-defense offering on the planet is a program called "Impact Model Mugging." Siciliano recommends you search for it online and find one near you He also recommends you bring your sons and daughters with you when you attend the course. In this case - as in most cases - knowledge is power.

4. You've heard this before and it requires revisiting: meet your date in a populated place and drive there yourself. And do it the same way at least for the first five times you meet. The goal here is you want to get to know the energy of this person and what makes them tick. If simple stuff irritates them or they make racist or offensive jokes or exhibit behaviors not conducive to "healthy" behavior - that's your signal to move on. And with your own transportation available, you can do so without any hassle or danger to yourself.

5. Do not consume alcohol when meeting, even

if you're taking it with food. This may seem harsh, or unrealistic when you're first getting to know someone. We get it. However, alcohol lowers our inhibitions and makes us exhibit and accept behaviors that aren't appropriate. Don't accept drinks from anyone under any condition unless you see the drink being poured and it goes straight into your hands and mouth. Slipping drugs in drinks happens every day - and you do not want to be the recipient. Correct?

6. Be direct about going 'Dutch' with regard to paying for dinner.

While this may seem extreme to some, studies show a large percentage of males still believe that when they buy a woman dinner, she "owes" him sex. Bam! Wrong answer! However, ladies: if this is what a man you're with might be assuming - we believe - he's not the man for you. You didn't sign up to be a prostitute.

Also, do NOT use sites like Craigslist, etc. and represent yourself as someone you may not be (or want to be). You may remember the masseuse in Boston who ended up being murdered by the med school student who was engaged and looked the part of the all-American blond, blue-eyed male. Didn't turn out that way, and we want to make sure nothing like that happens to you.

7. Take lots of pictures of the person you're with using your mobile phone, and mention you're emailing the photos to everyone in your life to show them who you are with and where you are.

We recommend doing this because it's never a bad idea to let a friend know who you're with, what their name is and where you'll be meeting them. It's likely that only someone with something to hide would be opposed to you doing this—so we say, "shoot" away! It can be done in a nice and friendly way, without making someone uncomfortable, but if it does annoy him or her, so be it. If they're that uncomfortable being photographed, they're probably hiding something - or want to be - and therefore, they're not for you!

8. Get as much information about the person as possible.

Think about this as market research for the intelligent consumer. As the relationship continues (past a couple of dates), you need to ask several questions. Obviously, you should get their name, address, previous address, home phone, cell phone, place of birth, birthdate, where they work, license plate, and if you can squeeze it out of them—and Siciliano kids you not about the need for this— get their Social Security number.

This is obviously tricky - as you might not want to share this same information about yourself with someone else. However, at the time of being in a committed relationship, this information should be shared with one another. Again, if you're not willing to share - or the person you're with is not - ask yourself, "what's there to hide?"

9. Go online and Google and search every bit of information about them you have acquired.

You want to know as much about this person as possible. Search name, phone, email and screen name. As you begin to "mine" this data, the deeper you dig the more you will find out about this person - the good, the bad and the occasional ugly. The goal is to look for truth and lies. If you see inconsistencies, or red flags that can't be easily explained - run, don't walk away. This is consumer fraud multiplied! Block them from the site and report them to the online site you found them on.

A background check is an entirely necessary tool that alerts you to any red flags or inconsistencies in their dialogue with you. Getting a background check done on a person is inexpensive, quick and smart. Sad, but true. You have to do what will protect you and your family and this is one sure way to do so.

Millions of people use online dating sites to broaden their networks and meet potential mates, but not everyone on these sites is sincere. Some are scammers hoping to lure you in with false affection, with the goal of gaining your trust, and eventually, your money.

NEIL: I found a profile of a beautiful young lady who lived about ten miles away from me. We emailed back and forth. She sent a few photos of herself in a bikini at the beach. I was interested and asked to talk on the phone. She was always too busy, but promised "sometime soon. A month later, she told me that she had fallen in love with me and would like to move in with me, although we had never met. She just needed $5,000 for her visa and plane ticket from Russia. I blocked and reported her, after telling her to get lost. Don't be swindled!

When seeking friends or dates via the Internet, people often tend to be overly optimistic or trusting, but it is important to remember that some people may take advantage of the your trust. Here are some tips for staying safe while making friends online.

• Keep your personal information just that: personal.

OK, we get that this is in conflict with what was said previously, so let's explain: Timing is everything, and asking for details about where he or she lives and works, their phone number(s) or email address(es), or details that would lead someone to where you are with minimal effort should NOT be put in an online profile or shared with someone you've barely started communicating with only recently.

When selecting a profile name, don't use your first and last name. Instead, choose a nickname or other title for yourself so that potential dates don't have the key information for looking you up and learning too much about you in advance. If you've started talking to someone you feel you would like to exchange personal information with, consider offering a secondary email account that isn't directly linked to you or your work (email addresses are free and nothing stops you from having more than one).

- Trust your gut and intuition. Use common sense and your instincts to stay away from risky situations. If something doesn't feel right, it's not right. If you feel nervous about someone or something, don't go; you probably feel that way for a reason. If the person is really interested in you, she or he won't hate you for rescheduling for a later time. Another part of trusting yourself is knowing what speed feels right for you. Don't feel obligated to go somewhere private or unfamiliar just because the other person wants to. Again, you know yourself best and you have enough life experience to know when something could end badly: listen to yourself.

- Meet new people in public. It seems obvious, but you

shouldn't bring total strangers back to your house (nor should you go to their homes or apartments). When scheduling a first meeting, plan to go somewhere public where a lot of people will be milling around. A park, restaurant, or museum can be great areas for public first dates, not only because they are public, but because they are places where you can actually talk to your date and get to know him or her in person.

• When you have a first date with someone, make sure that you are in control of your own transportation situation by driving yourself, taking a trusted form of transit, or arranging a ride with a good friend. Do NOT rely on your date to take you somewhere. Getting in a car with someone you barely know is not a great idea - ever. Look what has happened at shopping malls, etc. The same, sad to say, could happen to you as well. Be safe.

• Tell someone you trust where you are going. In case the worst does happen (it probably won't, but it never hurts to be prepared), make sure someone knows where you are going and when you expect to return home. Let a good friend know that you are going on a date with someone new and agree to check in with him/her by a certain time so they know you are OK. You might also set up a pickup spot in case you want your friend to pick you up if and when you need to bail on your date for any reason.

We're not trying to scare anyone out of meeting someone; however, we truly do want you to be safe. There are several "catfishes" out there, attempting to prey on innocent victims and we want to make sure you are in the safest situation possible. Keep your ears and eyes wide open for warning signs and be pro-active!

Online dating isn't all about being cynical and mistrusting. Most people are good, if not great people. You do need to take precautions when meeting someone new, however. Anyone who is worth getting to know will be empathetic to your safety concerns and willing to work with you within your comfort zone.

Stay tuned for warning signs - even ones you don't want to have to admit to or "see." What happens when you decide to meet someone and you begin to discover little white lies? Realize that little white lies are often a front for big darker lies. What else is this person hiding? Are they married, have kids? Have they gone bankrupt or been arrested for violence? Or, are they a registered sex offender? Are they unemployed, but told you they have a job?

Sometimes the truth hurts, and people innocently choose to adopt the "what they don't know won't hurt them" philosophy. But as the saying goes "the truth will set you free." You want to know as much about the good, the bad and the ugly as early on in the game as possible. Don't allow someone to gloss over, or not speak the truth. Nothing good can come of this. This is why it is essential that you do your homework and find out as much about this person as possible, to head off any potential future heart aches.

Siciliano likes to expose the flaws in our systems, and to find what makes certain individuals more vulnerable than others. Much of his "research" is prompted by his desire to learn more about the scumbags of society, who prey on others.

To that end, he's signed up for online dating sites, has created a profile as a woman, and waited for men to contact him. His research has led him to discover some particularly shady methods that scammers use to target emotionally vulnerable victims. The most common scam is an "advance fee" arrangement involving a wire transfer.

Here's a "perfect" example. A divorced mother of three in Britain was taken for 80,000 pounds by a scammer posing as a US soldier. It began when a man who called himself Sergeant Ray Smith introduced himself on a dating website. Soon they were chatting and emailing regularly, and then he was calling her on the phone and asking her to wire him money.

All over the world, online dating sites are riddled with Internet scammers. For example the Australian government has collected reports from 1600 Internet fraud victims who reported losing a total of $17 million to online dating scams in 2011.

We consider this an absolute atrocity. How could this be? **Siciliano** feels the same way, and says, "It blows me away that these scams are even possible!" In many of these cases, the same scammers maintain multiple profiles on different dating sites, and the dating sites do almost nothing to prevent or police this process.

In the last 90 days, 230,000 fraud and abuse attempts were reported from dating sites alone, including:
- Spamming - 90,000
- Scams and solicitations - 30,000
- Inappropriate content - 20,000
- Chat abuse - 17,000
- Profile misrepresentation - 15,000
- Credit card fraud - 14,000

- Identity mining / phishing attempts - 12,000

So, ladies and gentlemen -in order to protect your heart and your life, we suggest the following:

A Few Special Tips: Protecting Yourself from Scammers

- When signing up for online dating, go with a well-known dating site and get referrals from friends on which sites they use and why!
- Design your dating profile with care — think about the image you want to project and NEVER, under any circumstance, post personal information, such as your full name, address and phone number - we mean it!
- Vet potential dates by checking to see that their profile information matches other online information, such as their LinkedIn or Facebook profiles.
- If a potential date asks you for a loan or any financial information, immediately report them to the dating site - like right now! Do not send cash - ever! This is called catfishing and it's not wise, safe or worthwhile in any situation!
- NEVER EVER click on links in emails or eCards from people you do not know - if you don't trust it, DO NOT click it!

To help protect you from malware, use comprehensive security software, such as McAfee Total Protection, and keep it up-to-date by downloading new versions as soon as they become available.

The last word: Dating should be fun and exciting. However, there is a strong need in this day and age to be safe and not naïve.

Dating Success After 40

We wish you the best of luck and remember to have fun.

Just please, be safe about it!

Chapter 7

Image Does Matter

Ladies and Gents - image matters. You know the old saying, "you never have a second chance to make a first impression."

You simply have to step up your game in the appearance category if you want to land your man - or woman. OK, you probably think this is shallow and superficial. Say it isn't so. Bam! Wrong answer.

Your physical appearance and the way you present yourself online and offline are your personal brand and billboard to your ideal target market. Really!

If you don't believe us, check this out —Wikipedia defines nonverbal communication as representing:

> two-thirds of all communication…Nonverbal communication can portray a message both verbally and with the correct body signals. Body signals comprise physical features, conscious and unconscious gestures and signals, and the mediation of personal space…The wrong message can be established if the body language conveyed does not match a verbal message.
>
> Nonverbal communication strengthens a first impression in common situations like attracting a partner or in

a business interview: impressions are on average formed within the first four seconds of contact...First encounters or interactions with another person strongly affect a person's perception...When the other person or group is absorbing the message they are focused on the entire environment around them, meaning the other person uses all five senses in the interaction: 83% sight, 11% hearing, 3% smell, 2% touch and 1% taste.

Good marketers understand that looks matter, and they spend thousands on behalf of their clients to "position" them for success. If you've ever been in on the shoot of a product advertisement, you know about all this, but if you haven't -- well, you'd be shocked at the hours spent in advance preparation, attention to details on the day(s) of the actual shoot, plus the post-production editing, etc.

As single adults, we need to do the same - when it comes to positioning and "dressing up" the product, which is, of course, ourselves.

Marketing and sales people also need a back-up plan when, despite their best efforts to portray their client's product or service in the best light possible, something goes wrong. The model's outfit has a tear in it, the makeup person is a no-show, or the set design is in a different color and won't work with the other elements of the shoot chosen. You get the picture - it's Murphy's Law ("Whatever can go wrong, will go wrong.") So, when the inevitable happens, what do they do? They go to Plan B, with quick adjustments to make it work. The key is to be prepared.

Moving beyond the proven fact that looks do matter, as do first impressions - it's also important to focus on some other...eh, hmm, more important and intimate details - like good grooming.

This may seem like an obvious one, but trust us - we've seen more of our fair share of less-than-good grooming among some of our dates.

It's our intention to be sensitive here, but some things simply need to be said. So...

Here are some good grooming habits we recommend to both genders:

- Be clean - daily showers are a must, and we suggest one prior to a date (even if you've already taken one in the morning). Cleanliness is next to "Date-Worthiness" in our book.

- Wear clean clothes - never use the "sniff" test to see if your clothing is clean and worth wearing on a date - whether it's the first one or the ninth one. We have a friend who is in love with her boyfriend - except for one thing - he consistently shows up wearing clothes with stains on them. This causes significant hesitation whenever she is faced with the possibility of being social or going out in public with her man, as well as being intimate. Nothing can kill a hot night more than bad behavior and unconscious non-grooming.

- Have clean hair - do you see a theme here? What does it take to wash your hair while in the shower - five more minutes? We think that's a worthwhile investment of your time. Your date — as well as society— will appreciate the effort. If you have a dandruff problem, talk to a dermatologist and be sure you're using shampoo and conditioner that can assist you in combatting the problem.

- Have good dental hygiene. We're talking regular dental appointments with cleaning, brushing and flossing, and if you're missing teeth - please replace them. We realize this is a costly endeavor - to maintain good dental health, but honestly, it's a worthwhile investment in you and your future overall health. At a minimum, brushing and flossing is a must. Be sure to have fresh breath as well. Keep breath mints in your car and on your person at all times.

- Nail care is also a major consideration. We will see our date's hands throughout our interactions including eating, speaking (for those who are particularly expressive), touching, intimacy/sex - you get it? Be sure to have clean, trimmed and filed nails - men and women alike. Women may want to have professional manicures or can do their names themselves with polish, etc. Beware the "dragon lady" look, though, with extensively long nails. Let's leave that to the porn sites - unless it's a special request from your love interest and you don't mind the added length on nails.

- Be sure to wear deodorant or antiperspirant. Nothing is more distasteful or embarrassing than body odor of any kind. Underarm scents are particularly potent and unpleasant - and, sometimes, may not be recognizable to the person who has them. If you're doing a physical activity together, make arrangements for a quick follow-up shower and keep these essential grooming items in your car or with you.

- Pay attention to the details of your clothing, shoes, and accessories. Take the time to polish your shoes, repair them if necessary - or toss them if they're in rough shape and unfixable. When we pay attention to the details in how we present ourselves, it gives the people around us a sense that we are capable, competent and take care of ourselves and our lives. Ladies and gentleman, please: no damaged clothing, non-matching socks (to pants), scuffed shoes, runs in stockings and un-ironed clothing items. Taking the time to take care of your clothing and accessories prior to the date shows respect for yourself and your date.

NANCY: For you Ladies, we have a few gender-specific considerations when it comes to good grooming. Most women post-40 are entering a new era, and can be at any point from peri-menopause to full-blown menopause. Welcome to the club. With this come potentially embarrassing moments of unexpected breakthrough bleeding, extreme hot flashes and perspiration, moments of being unable to remember or come up with the "right" word for certain things, among other uncomfortable or embarrassing symptoms.

In order to avoid - or at a minimum keep these potentially embarrassing moments under control, be sure to always have the following on hand - or in your car:

- Tampons
- Panty liners/pads
- Hormone creams/pills (if they've been prescribed for you)
- Fresh facecloth in a re-sealable plastic bag - for a quick clean up and storage of dirty item(s)
- Mild soap
- Body splash/cologne (nothing too heavy or overpowering)

- Tooth brush, dental floss, breath mints, deodorant/anti-perspirant
- Extra pair of panties/underpants
- Extra pair of pantyhose
- Dark pants/slacks or skirt
- Bottle of water (in case there's none available)
- Adult wipes (really!)

As the Boy Scouts' motto, "Be Prepared," states, it's always better to be safe than sorry. If any potentially embarrassing moment happens, if you're armed with the items you need to simply take care of it - you'll be far less stressed than if you didn't have them.

For you Gents: Here are some items you may want to carry in your car, just in case:

- Fresh facecloth in a re-sealable plastic bag - for a quick clean up and storage of dirty item(s)
- Mild soap
- Body splash/cologne (nothing too heavy or overpowering)
- Tooth brush, dental floss, breath mints, deodorant/antiperspirant
- Extra pair of underwear
- Bottle of water (in case there's none available)
- Adult wipes (really!)

Here's the other great thing about being a more mature single that is dating again - we get it. We're all adults here and have had experiences ourselves, with our ex-spouses, or other dates that we've had to deal with, be empathic about and, quite frankly, get over these "issues" ideally with some grace and ease.

The key is to realize that good grooming is a great start, and being prepared for the "unexpected" grooming issues is icing on the proverbial cake.

Now let's talk about clothing and what to wear on dates. Before we get into specifics, keep the following expert tips in mind.

When it comes to dressing for a date, post-40, **Kimberly Seltzer**, **of Elite Image Makeovers**, offers the following advice:

Dress The Part - many of my clients over 40 find themselves stuck in a rut still wearing clothes from the 90's or wearing work clothes on their dates. Figuring out how to dress to attract the opposite sex is no easy task, but if you dress in a way that makes you look and feel confident then you know you are on the right track.

For women, your primary focus should be to dress in a feminine way that honors your figure. As we get older women's bodies change so it's important to know your body type and emphasize the parts you love and deemphasize the parts you want to conceal in order to feel confident. When choosing your outfit and thinking about key essentials, keep in mind that men love women in dresses, skirts, jewelry and heels. And don't forget about the details! Have your nails well manicured, wear makeup and style your hair so it's flowing. Your goal for the first date is to appear mysterious, feminine and approachable. Make sure you're not showing too much skin or dressing provocatively. Remember that sexiness is a result of creating intrigue and curiosity.

For men, don't underestimate the power of your clothes with the ladies! In fact, the number one thing that most women find attractive is a man who looks put together and successful. I've peeked in many men's closets that are still filled with acid washed jeans, pleated pants and baseball jerseys from the days of old…not a sexy look when trying to attract that special woman today. Make sure you update your wardrobe by getting clothes that are youthful, fit your body well and have a unique personal style that suits you. Impress her by looking casually stylish with a few of these staples: a pair of well fitted jeans, a stylish shirt, leather jacket and clean shoes or boots.

Ginger Burr, **of Total Image Consultants**, agrees that dating post-40 offers some additional clothing challenges and provides the following tips:

- Don't wear your work clothes on a date. You want to look like you have a life outside of work and date clothes are generally more fun than clothes you wear to the office. Plus, there is a psychological component to wearing different clothes—you feel like you are switching gears from work to play!
- Don't wear the same old pair of jeans or clothes you wear hanging around the house. You want to feel special, beautiful and self-confident. Choose clothes that make you smile and feel good about yourself when you put them on.
- Be prepared. Presumably, you will attract someone who enjoys doing some of the same things you do, so you want to be ready for those experiences. Whether it's going to a ballgame, on a picnic, to the symphony or salsa dancing, you will need a varied wardrobe. And, you don't want to shop out of desperation the night before a date!

Now, keep those expert tips in mind as you read

the following discussions **for both women and men**, **on exactly what to wear, and what to toss**, from your closet before you head out the door for a date.

NANCY: **For you Ladies**, let's start with a few basic ideas on basics to have in your wardrobe:

- Great pair of jeans. They must fit you perfectly, be long enough (jeans worn too short ruin an outfit. Long enough means that if they are straight leg or boot-cut they should be no more than 1/2 inch off the ground, and if they are a skinny jean, they need to cover your ankles), and preferably dark wash or black. No baggy jeans or mom jeans!
- A great top. Notice I didn't say a T-shirt. Skip the T-shirt in favor of a pretty casual top. One style that looks great on a lot of women is a faux wrap top. It has a flattering neckline (if it's too low, wear a cami under it) and flatters your curves!
- A cardigan or jacket. Whether you choose a cardigan or jacket is up to you, but you will generally want something in case the weather turns cool. It could be a traditional cardigan — although be wary of crewneck cardigans with a band at the bottom. They can look frumpy. Choose one with a scoop or V-neck. A great jean jacket is very handy and you can get it in a traditional blue (choose one in a different shade of blue from your jeans!) or in white or a color.
- Pretty shoes. This does not mean they have to have a high heel - in fact, that can (especially if it's not your general way of dressing) feel out of place at a ball game or picnic. But, don't settle for clunky sneakers. Choose a pair of sandals, shoes or boots (if it's a spring or fall outing) that make you feel sexy without looking out of place.
- Beautiful lingerie. Even if he isn't going to see it, you know you are wearing it and not only will you feel beautiful

and sexy, but your clothes will fit better with well-fitting undergarments.

- If jeans aren't your thing, go for a pretty sundress or a skirt and top.

For a dinner date at a nice restaurant, choose:

- A dress. One that hits at the knee or 3-4 inches above (depending how much leg you feel comfortable showing) always looks sexy and flattering. It can be your version of a little black dress, but it doesn't have to be black! It can be any color that looks gorgeous on you. Choose a deeper color (eggplant, deep teal or navy, for example) and it will feel timeless and elegant. Keep the design simple and you can dress it up or down with accessories.
- A great pair of pants and a beautiful top. If it isn't a dressy restaurant, you can even choose a pair of well-fitting black jeans with sexy shoes or boots. Choose a top in a gorgeous color that frames your face well. Avoid crew neck tops - they are unflattering on most people.

Always be you! As I was helping a client (who was in her late 30's and hadn't dated for over 15 years) get ready to get back into the dating scene, I could tell that she was nervous. She wanted men to find her attractive and she was worried she wouldn't do it right. She was a very quiet, gentle woman and had one big concern: when was she supposed to show cleavage on a date? Was it the first date? Second? Third?

Sensing her discomfort, I asked her how she felt about showing cleavage. She said that she didn't usually show a lot of it because she felt exposed and uncomfortable when she did. I then asked her why she felt she had to. She looked at me with surprise and said, "Don't they expect it?"

The question then came down to one that we've mentioned so frequently in this book: her target market. Whom was she trying to attract? Were the men who expected her to show lots of exposed skin the kind of man she wanted to date?

No. She was so relieved! I explained that she could look

and feel sexy without exposing anything she didn't want to. The goal was for her to look and feel radiant. She enjoyed wearing skirts and pretty shoes and that felt sexy to her and, I suggested, would also attract more of the men with whom she wanted to spend time.

If you try to be someone else or someone you think you're supposed to be, you will not attract the men who are naturally drawn to the real you! Plus, you will feel stressed and exhausted keeping up appearances, so to speak. Eventually, if the relationship goes anywhere, you will have to expose whom you really are anyway, and you don't want that to be a complete surprise! Dress in a way that makes you feel beautiful and sexy, and the right men will find you beautiful and sexy, too!

NEIL: OK, **Gents**, we aren't leaving you out. In fact, we consulted an expert and she had lots of great advice to share!

Emmi Sorokin, of the website **National Image Consultant for Men**, specializes in men's casual style. Asked for tips on how men should dress for dates, Emmi shared the following:

There is an epidemic of hidden hot men in this country — men who, with just a few tweaks in garment choice, will look infinitely more desirable. It's no secret women care at a core level about aesthetics, but that doesn't mean they are shallow and won't like you for you. The vessel that carries the soul mate is important and all humans appreciate good packaging.

Imagine you're seated at a bar and the bartender pours you two glasses of your favorite beer; one glass is sparkling and clean and the second glass has smudges and a chip. Any guy would go for the nicer looking glass. The same basic human nature applies in the dating scene.

What scares a lot of men off from tackling their dating wardrobe is that they think in order to be better dressed they need to start dressing fancier, uncomfortably or somehow not true to themselves. This is a complete fallacy. What men really want is to feel completely confident and to look effortless in their style, and the solution is simply to wear a comfortable, body-flattering outfit that feels great and works for the setting. I'll explain how easy it is to do just that, but first let's take a look at the very common mistakes that good men make that have them get passed over.

- Do Not Wear ANYTHING Baggy.
  Your goal is to look masculine, which means no matter your body's size, shape, or height, you always want your shoulders to be the most prominent part of your physique. It's your strong man-shoulders that your date is going to envision snuggling into as you tell her about where you're originally from, and if she can't picture that, it ain't happening and you're going in the friend zone.

  A shirt that's even a bit too large will droop off your shoulders and pull the attention away from your shoulder line to the excess fabric bunching around your midsection making you appear frumpy and sloppy.

  Below-the-waist fit is just as important. Whether you're wearing jeans or trousers, if you need a belt to keep them up they are too big.

- In the mood for a good pun? Good, because here comes one with my next tip: do not date yourself.

If what you are considering wearing to meet your hopefully spark-filled connection is more than a few years old, it's time to update. The goal is to look current, not 'in fashion.' Men tend to keep stuff in their closets way past the expiration date and not get new items when needed. Remember that what you wear tells people plenty about you before you even open your mouth. What does a faded mock turtleneck say? Nothing that's going to attract someone to you.

- Don't overdo it trying to show your fun side by wearing loud colors or crazy prints. Bright primary colors like yellow and orange, anything with skulls, dragons, or giant crosses (we're lookin' at you, Ed Hardy) and party prints like Hawaiian shirts end up wearing you instead of the other way around. For the majority of men, bright colors and bold patterns work best on a small scale in accessories. Show your fun side with your personality and by how you make her feel in your presence.

- Don't advertise your athlete's foot by wearing gym sneakers. Instead, go with a pair of casual sneakers. There are plenty on the market that are just as comfortable as New Balance, that will also look great with denim or any casual pant.

- No white gym socks with anything. Your socks should either be an extension of your leg and be in the same color range as your pant or be purposefully distinctive, like a bold color stripe or fun plaid.

- Don't mistake your date for an interview. Office clothing, by design, does not set the tone for intimacy. Dates are not business casual, they're usually dressy casual. That means richer fabrics like cashmere, soft-brushed cottons, and tweeds, and richer colors like emerald and deep blue.

- Don't do either of these canned-and-stored-too-long-in-the-suburbs looks: the untucked dress shirt & jeans or the tucked in polo into Dockers, especially with the crowning cherry on the sad sundae, a baseball cap. These styles favored heavily in the late 90's and the last thing you want to do is give the impression that you haven't mixed things up since then.

- Don't roll out in dad jeans! If you don't know what those are, google image search them and then look in the mirror. If there is even a slight resemblance in fit or wash, it's time to upgrade your denim. It will not matter if you spend $30 or $300 on your jeans; all that counts is that they fit you great and have a modern wash.

Now that we've covered what doesn't work, let's jump into what does:

Start with the foundation of a properly groomed and manscaped body (shower, shave if no beard, nose hair and ear hair clipped, and fingernails short and clean). You can then create the perfect look for yourself for any occasion in just four steps. I call it The "Style 4mula." It's the DNA of effortless style. Any time you see someone who looks pulled together, it's because they've nailed these four elements.

- **Fit:** The foundation of good style. Without nailing the fit, no matter how nice or expensive the garment is, you won't look good. Evolutionary psychology has taught all of us that the most desirable feminine silhouette is hourglass and a man's is a V shape. That means no matter how you are dressed your shoulders should be the widest part of your physique to emphasize that V, and it all starts with clothing that fits your body well.

For any shirt start checking for fit at the shoulders. The shoulder seams should never extend past the slope of your shoulder because that seam also determines how wide the body is. The moment it drops off your shoulder you'll kill your strong shoulder line and look wider and droopy.

From below your armpit the shirt should glide along your body, never billowing away because it's too loose or bunching in the small of your back because it's too tight.

Fit is just as important below the belt, and for your pants the fabric should skim your legs and backside without any excess fabric cascading down or gathering at the ankle.

- **Feel:** Every garment sets a different tone, and to look good, what you're wearing has to make sense for your age, your personality, and the occasion. For example, two pairs of jeans can have very different feels. A dark dress denim will feel right at a romantic restaurant with a blazer and dress shoes, whereas light blue or color denim has a more casual feel and would be better with a polo and boat shoes or a t-shirt and loafers.

  There are casual dates and dressier dates, so think about the formality of the date you're going into and try to have a couple of options for each type.

  For casual/sportier dates you could do a casual button down with the sleeves rolled up, a light color great-fitting jean, a suede or woven fabric belt, and a driving moc or other nice loafer.

Or you could do a fitted color t-shirt underneath a well-cut cashmere zip hoodie, a grey chino, and a suede boot.

For dressier occasions you could do a blazer that was designed to be worn with dress denim, a patterned dress shirt and nicely fitting cardigan, and a color wingtip shoe.

Alternatively, you could opt for a shawl neck cardigan with a button down, dress slacks, and a loafer.

- **Layering**: Most men think of an outfit in 2 pieces (a top and a bottom), but just like in a *ménage a trois*, a look comes together when there are 3 pieces in play - two tops and a bottom. So start thinking of a look as a bottom, a top, and a top-finishing piece. A well-chosen finishing layer - whether hoodie or casual blazer - elevates your look, creates character and depth, and helps reinforce the masculine silhouette. For example, if you're a guy with more around the middle, wearing a tailored casual blazer will subtly accentuate your shoulders while also narrowing your waist.

- **Accessories**: Accessories are your secret weapon, not only because they pull your whole look together, but also because they can cut your social efforts in half. Women will always comment on and appreciate well-chosen accessories; they show that you pay attention to details, and that's very attractive.

  A grey belt goes with any color and is a refreshing alternative to the traditional brown or black. Statement socks in fun colors and prints add some spice to denim or any pant. A pocket square for a casual blazer or tailored vest feels more elegant than a tie. Color shoelaces suddenly make a so-so shoe look cool.

When you nail the right fit, feel, top layer, and accessories, you'll have an effortless confidence that people are naturally drawn to, and that is the whole reason behind learning to dress well.

If you still feel uncertain about styling yourself, that's okay. Men's styles have changed quite a bit in recent years and every man's body is different and flattered by select cuts, styles, and colors. Take the time to learn yours because the investment pays off! Either ask a trusted friend with good taste, or better, hire a skilled image consultant who can create a few head-to-toe looks you'll love in less time than it will take you to find a shirt.

Chapter 8

Mind Your Manners

We might be putting the cart before the horse here, but we believe it's important to brush up on dating etiquette *before* you actually have your first date. Manners do matter: they're an integral part of the social process of life we're all engaged in - from entertaining a client at a fine restaurant or a casual lunch spot, to attempting to woo a partner into our lives.

Like it or not, people are watching you and making judgments based on your dining habits, personal grooming, overall politeness, and the level of empathy and consideration you show yourself and the people around you.

There are some obvious etiquette blunders that in our opinion should be avoided when on a date.

Call us crazy, but we're more of a traditional mindset when it comes to dating protocol.

NANCY: Personally, I like/love a chivalrous man - bring him on! I want someone to open the door for me - starting with the car door, to the restaurant, coffee shop, or wherever we might go. Yes, I'm independent and happy to take care of myself. However, when I'm in the company of a man - I want to feel not alone, but protected and cared for. I'm happy to do the same for him in other situations that may be more traditional, like making dinner or bringing a treat I made for him to enjoy. I'd be happy to be on the receiving end of that as well.

Who pays? I totally appreciate a man paying on the first date. After that, I'm happy to kick-in and treat my date. What I'd prefer not to do is go "Dutch," and split the bill. It takes all of the romance out of the experience, in my opinion.

I also like when a man walks on the outside (the curb side) when we're walking down a street. Then, too, I appreciate a man who, once he's opened a door for me, gently places his hand on my back to guide me in.

And I'm rather blown away by gentlemanly behavior in a restaurant. My ideal man allows me to sit facing out to the crowd and pulls my seat out for me. Once, I was looking for a seat at a business luncheon meeting in Boston, and I finally spotted a table consisting entirely of gentlemen. As I approached and asked if I could take the only remaining seat available, one of the men stood up as I was seated. I almost fainted. I was also very impressed.

As I observed everyone at that table, I also noticed the impeccable table manners of this particular gentleman. He waited until I was seated and had taken the first bite of this amazing lunch before he started to eat. The way he held his eating utensils, chewed his food, and his overall mannerisms were a major turn-on for me. Had this man been single and asked me out - I would have said YES immediately.

Now, turning from the sublime to the less-than-enchanting, there are some obvious turn-offs when first meeting a man or woman, including, but not limited to:

Bad table manners

- Using utensils incorrectly
- Not using a napkin correctly - keep it on your lap and use when necessary.
- Picking your teeth at the table (excuse yourself and go to the restroom with a toothpick or dental floss instead)
- Reaching across people to "grab" items such as bread, butter, cream or sugar
- Buttering an entire piece of bread instead of breaking the bread and buttering each piece individually, etc.

There are plenty of excellent books and resources on proper manners. We're big fans of such how-to books. They offer you a quick and easy way to learn proper etiquette; if it wasn't something you were taught at home growing up, or at school or on the job. Not to worry - you're an adult now and these skills can be learned.

Because this is a dating book with a sales and marketing spin to it, we emphasize that good table manners are essential for both business and personal "selling" purposes.

According to **Roseanne Thomas,** a **Certified Business Etiquette Consultant and CEO of Protocol Advisors, INC.**, there are differences to be aware of between a business and social dining.

Here are some of **Roseanne's** takeaways about how each are unique and should be recognized and treated as such: Social and business dining differ because the basis of each relationship is different. In business dining there is typically an imbalance of power and an agenda for the meal. Generally, hosting in business situations puts the entire burden on the host. The choice of the restaurant, topics of discussion, paying of the bill, etc., all fall on the host, because he/she has a specific goal in mind that will ultimately benefit him/her. It could be making a new business acquaintance, furthering a business relationship, asking for advice, leads, introductions, intelligence or contracts, or generating goodwill among employees, colleagues or clients.

A guest in a business dining situation is not expected to pay any part of the bill, is not necessarily responsible for holding up 50% of the conversation (although it would be nice) and is not judged for charm, wit, attractiveness, generosity, dress, grooming, athleticism, altruism, etc. A business guest is also not required to reciprocate.

Unlike social dining, business dining is generally a means to an end and is not based upon shared interests and values, age, gender, goals, life stages, affection or hopes for a more personal relationship.

Business dining does not require deference across genders, nor is this recommended. Men do not need to seat women, open car doors, stand when they get up from the table, order for them, pay the bill (if the women have done the inviting) or walk them to their cars. Language or topics of conversation do not need to be modified for women, although it is highly recommended that language and topics be suitable in general.

NANCY: I guess I have to disagree a bit on this last item. As I mentioned previously, that guy at the business luncheon had me the moment he stood up when I asked to join the table. OK, now back to Roseanne's great advice:

Social dining, whether dating, or among friends and family, is predicated upon mutual affection or the hope for such. Everyone is on his or her best behavior, evidencing as many positive personal qualities as possible to encourage the growth of or deepening of a personal relationship.

At the outset of a dating relationship, it is incumbent upon the person who extended the invitation, whether a man or a woman, regardless of age, to pay for the excursion. The person who issued the invitation is not responsible for the other's transportation, although if travelling together is more practical, either may offer.

In social dining situations, it is very nice if a man does open the car door, extends an arm across uneven terrain and pulls out a chair for a woman, even if she has issued the invitation. Ordering for a woman is not often done (or appreciated) anymore, even in social situations, unless the order is for dishes to be shared.

The invitee at the first date does not have to offer to pay. The one who extended the invitation grabs the check immediately, and accepts no offer of splitting the bill or leaving the tip, etc.

While it is always more elegant if the person who invites pays entirely, with subsequent dates, some people say they like an offer to pay the bill or split the check, even if they do not accept. But I think it is always better, whether out to dinner, at a movie, or at home for a home-cooked dinner, that one person take the role as host and see to all aspects of the event.

Sooner than later, the one who has been entertained must reciprocate, as he/she is able.

Among some friends and relatives, it may be presumed that all will pay their own way. That is fine, unless it is a special event to celebrate a birthday, graduation, etc. In these cases, the honoree should not be allowed to pay, even if he/she offers.

We also spoke with **Jodi R. R. Smith, President of Mannersmith Etiquette Consulting,** who kindly offered the following advice and FAQ's:

Q. Who pays the bill (first date and beyond)?

A. Modern manners are surprisingly egalitarian. Whoever does the asking does the paying. Now, occasionally the woman may have done the asking, but the man prefers to do the paying. If he offers and she declines, he should allow her to pay. If he insists, she may opt to demure and allow him to pay. (Often this is a sign that the man is chivalrous, which may count in his favor.) On the other side of the coin, there are times when the man has done the asking and the woman insists on paying for the entire meal or her half of the bill. The man has the option of insisting he pay, or allowing her to pay half. (Often this is a sign that the date has NOT gone well and the woman is not interested.)

Q. Should women expect to have the door opened for them (car, restaurant)?

A. Chivalrous behavior, when not exhibited to the point of being controlling, can be a lovely way of showing both interest and respect. If a woman prefers a man with chivalrous behavior, she should be quite open about it. "You know, I certainly am happy to pay for dinner and dates here and there, but I just could not abide by my last boyfriend's habit of thinking that unlocking the car doors by remote was the same as him opening the car door. So tacky."

Q. Where does the man position himself, relative to the woman, when walking on a sidewalk, etc.?

A. In the olden days the man would stand between the woman and traffic to protect her from wayward carriages and the splash of muddy roads. It is a nice sign for respect to do so, but certainly not a manners-deal-breaker.

Q. What's appropriate clothing on a first, second or third date?

A. Depends on the date! Always, pressed and polished, whether that is khakis and a golf shirt or a cocktail dress. Whatever you think the attire is for that particular activity/venue, take it up a notch. It is better to show you thought too much of the person instead of not enough. Plus, even if this date may not be a love-connection, you never know who may be on the greens, in the bar, or visiting the lobby during intermission.

Q. When is it OK to be intimate on a date?

A. As an adult, your intimacy time-line is dependent upon you. If you are Ok with a first date also being a one-night-stand, then on the first date is fine. Otherwise, it is better to see if this person is a mental/emotional match before testing the waters. Certainly there needs to be some chemistry, so a goodnight kiss on the lips or some hot-and-heavy making out might be fun. Most daters do like a little bit of flirting and the excitement of the "thrill-of-the-chase." Getting to the bedroom too quickly can bring the game to a premature close.

Of course, manners matter, but safety first. Be sure to use appropriate protection. While pregnancy may no longer be your highest concern, there are certainly many other issues, which can be shared during intimate times.

Table etiquette — dos and don'ts.

Oh, where to start…I could write an entire book on this topic alone…

Here are my Top 10 Tips:

1. Be sure to find out if your date has any allergies or strong food preferences in advance. (It's bound to be a tough date when you bring a vegan to a steak restaurant and he orders just a baked potato.)

2. Choose a place that is lively for a good background vibe, but not so frenetic that you have to shout to be heard. Restaurants with a view provide a ready topic of conversation if needed. ("What a beautiful sunset!")

3. Opt to sit kitty-corner instead of across the table from one another. Across the table makes the date feel more like a job interview. (Avoid sitting in a booth during the first few dates. Later, when you do, sit on the same side… much more romantic!) 4. The date-host (the person who did the asking and will do the paying) should be clear about cue and clues for the meal. ("I'm going to have a glass of wine, would you care for a drink as well?")

5. The date-guest should maintain the symmetry of dining. If the host orders a salad, you should too. (It's weird to sit there and watch her eat a salad when you have nothing in front of you. And, it's very uncomfortable for her to be staring at you while you clumsily try to eat your salad and there's nothing in front of her.)

6. Choose items that are easy to eat if you're nervous.

Avoid French onion soup, any crustaceans in their shells, long pastas you will need to twist, or anything with many small bones. Opt instead for boneless breast of chicken, a fish which has been filleted, or pasta you can slice, such as lasagna.

7. Dinners can be long if you do not click easily at the start. Be sure to arrive with some back-up small talk topics. Ask your close friends which of your life history stories to share and which to avoid. Have some open ended questions at the ready to ask your date. (But be sure to avoid sounding like an interviewer.)

8. Mind you manners: small bites, chew with your mouth shut, pace yourself, use your utensils and your napkin.

9. When resting, your fork is on the left side of your plate between 11 and 8; your knife is on the right side between 1 and 4. When finished, your fork and knife are parallel on the right side of your plate. (These silent signals help both the wait staff and your date to know where you are in the mea10. Arrange in advance to have the bill come directly to you. Have your credit card at the ready so there is no need for the awkwardness of the bill at the end of the meal.

How to follow-up on a date when you're interested in continuing the relationship? And, when you're not?

Ah, the zing when the date went well; our hearts flutter with the hope of another. But, how to make sure the other person knows? This is one of the few times in life when being passive-aggressive works in our favor. You want to reach out, signal that you are interested, without actually engaging them in a conversation. A day (or two) after the date, leave a message where they are not. For example, if you know the person is at work, call the home number and leave a quick voicemail. If the person is not logged into Facebook or the dating website, type a quick message. Remember, the message needs to be quick, light and upbeat. "Your wit made me laugh so much I thought I was going to be escorted out of the gallery opening." "Thank you for encouraging me to try Thai food, it's great to know I do like yellow curry." Then allow the person the time and space to respond.

Of course, if they initiated the first date, you can initiate the second. A few days after the date, invite the person out. If they are busy, but offer an alternative get together, there is interest. If they are busy and are short during the call, there was not a connection.

If you are not interested, do not initiate contact. If they contact you, you should be kind and concise: "Ah, Pat…you are so sweet to ask me out again. While I enjoyed meeting you, we are not a good fit long term. I do wish you the best. Good bye." Please note, never elaborate on how you are not a good fit. It is cruel for you to list their failings, and mentioning your own allows them the opportunity for rebuttal. "Pat, you know my obsession-level hobby following the Star Trek conventions around the country. I could not subject a non-sci-fi fan to such a lifestyle." Rebuttal: "Yes, I may not like Star Trek, but I do like you and it would be a great chance for me to see the country."

How to say goodnight? Plan for next steps — or not?

I liken the exit strategy to those of stand-up comedians. If a comedian has a 10-minute set on stage, but gets a great laugh at the 6-minute mark, he exits the stage. Always leave on a high note, and always leave them

Dating Success After 40

wanting more. Don't wait for the date to drag to an awkward conclusion; rather, end the date after the activity, but before you run out of things to say. Do not plan for another date quite yet (you may not have kissed him/her yet) and while it is good to be enthusiastic, you do not want to appear over-eager. Sleep on it, and then plan for next steps.

Manners matter, but safety first: For the first few dates, you should meet and depart from public locations. Better a kiss under the streetlight than a dangerous situation at your front door.

Chapter 9

Setting Up Meetings Low Cost, High End Marketing Ideas for Memorable Dates

Yay! You've got a . . . date! Way to go! High five us! We know it's not always easy - regardless of how you meet someone, so let's just say - we're psyched for you.

First dates can be very exciting, and the preceding few days before you actually meet can make your mind swirl. So many people ask us what we suggest they do for a first date. We always encourage them to do something they will both enjoy but won't eat up (so to speak) an entire day or evening - at least to start. If your date turns out to be with someone you'd like to extend your time with - you can always ask.

NANCY: I prefer meeting for coffee. I settled on this as the best venue for a first-time date after one too many meetings that went awry — and ended up with me spending way too many hours sitting across from someone I had nothing in common with. It was just too much, or too long a time to be with someone before figuring out whether or not I'd like to get to know him better - or not so much.

NEIL: I live at the beach, so anyone that enjoys walking or running on the coast usually loves a walk on the beach. That has been the place for my first date most of the time. I've also met for coffee, lunch or dinner, of course. The first date should allow you both to have a conversation and get to know each other.

NANCY: Neil loves to brag about living at the beach - yadda, yadda, yadda. I happen to live in a historic and picturesque town filled with ponds, parks and paths. A walk on a nice day and a cup of coffee is a great way to test the waters and strike up a conversation with someone.

As I mentioned earlier, meeting for a cup of coffee or lunch is a quick, easy and inexpensive way to see if you two have any chemistry.

On the other hand, ahem, Nancy will skip dinner. Frankly, we know plenty of women (I hate to admit, as a woman myself) who "use" men as a meal ticket and honestly, it's deplorable. Don't do it - you'll pay for it in the end if you do.

Who pays for what, then, you wonder? Please check our list of do's and don'ts on first dates in Chapter 8, on etiquette. Neil is a traditionalist and always pays on the first date. I have to admit that I like that. Even though I have no problem paying for future dates and adventures together, I feel that the first date sets the tone, and women (still, I believe) like to feel like a woman.

If a man is gracious enough to pick up the check on the first date, his chances of landing a second one increase. It's not the only reason, of course, but I have actually sat through long meals and seen checks sit on the table long enough that I just happily paid— and never saw the dude again. One date asked me when the check arrived, "What do you think is fair?" Please — don't do that! If the guy doesn't pay for this first date, you may want to keep searching through the other hundreds of potential matches.

Whether or not you want to do dinner on a first date, it is often a great idea for a subsequent meeting, once you know you would like to spend a couple hours with each other. Sharing a meal offers a wonderful opportunity to get to know each other on a deeper level.

Anthony Ambrose, a very successful chef and restaurant owner in the Boston area, offers these tips on dining and learning about your date:

Listening skills are key in every aspect, but especially with food. Ask your date about likes and dislikes, allergy issues and food preferences. If you are dining out, select a restaurant with a good vibe, ambiance and comfortable environment that matches his/her personality. You want to be able to speak to and hear each other during dinner. Select a cuisine that your guest will be comfortable with and can understand the menu and choices.

You can learn a lot about a date at the table. How do they act in public? Are they polite and respectful to the waitress, waiter and hostess? If the meal isn't cooked as preferred, how do they roll?

Anthony also provides tips for "dining in" at home:

Making dinner for your date is very romantic. Cooking together, cutting and touching the vegetables and prepping everything to create a colorful and delicious salad, creates a romantic bond. You can use exotic curries and spices that you can break down to pull out the cinnamons and use an infused oil before sautéing the garlic. Freshly ground star anise is something you can sprinkle into the oil and watch it boil before you put in a seared pork loin, for example. It smells delicious in the kitchen.

Egyptians and Indians used these ingredients as 'romance enhancing spices' that were handed down by generation over centuries. Use vanilla bean and chocolate to finish the meal, since they are clean, delicate and perfumy to accentuate the experience and rules of romance. Creating a meal together like this is fun and you can't really make a mistake.

There are many other great ideas for a date, as well, that don't include the traditional dinner or movie. Be creative and open to fun, unique and maybe new experiences. Going for a walk through a park is also a quiet place to talk, enjoy the fresh air and get to know each other, especially if you are both outdoorsy. This isn't something a high-maintenance woman or a lazy man would embrace, however.

NANCY: Note to Neil (you crazy runner, hiker, biker dude): As women, we get that this is what most men want - someone who is "active." News flash! We do too. I may be mistaken, but I read this in far more male profiles (the request to be physically fit and active) than I do in the section of women's profiles outlining the qualities they desire in a man. Although I'm not as physically driven as Neil - I definitely support the idea that it's important to have a balance of your wishes in a partner, and not be too focused on primarily one thing.

I love movies, but I think it's not a great thing to do on a first date. Maybe not a second or third date either - while you're getting to know someone.

It's always better to be safe than sorry, as spelled out in the chapter on security and safety. Be sure you meet in a public place, of course, since you don't know each other yet. Some of our friends have met at museums to view the artwork.

NEIL: OMG, I'd be bored to tears. That's definitely not my idea of a fun date, but if that's your thing, then have fun. This is why it's good to be open to new things and people who might have interests they can share with you as well.

Bowling is also something different to enjoy. If you have never bowled or haven't in a while, a first date at a bowling alley could create a scene for many laughs and plenty of fun. The two of you can enjoy a drink, have a sandwich and some friendly competition, if you like. If things go well, then maybe a light dinner or a drink will follow.

I've not seen Nancy bowl - and she tells me I should be thankful for that. But, for those of you who are more coordinated than Nancy - go for it and send us your video footage.

Some first-timers go to wine-tastings as a way to mingle with others, get to know each other, have fun and see how the date is in a social situation. Match.com even has "meet ups" - called Stir Events. I took a first date to a Stir Event in a private kitchen, just a few miles from our homes. Everyone learned to make tapas, have wine and mingle. It was casual, inexpensive and fun! We think this is a brilliant idea, as nothing replaces that face-to-face meeting. It also takes the pressure off a "real date" situation.

NANCY: I'm a fan of 8-Minute Dating, a unique concept that allows you to meet several people consecutively. You spend eight minutes talking with each person before moving on to the next potential "match." I found many of the men to be interesting, funny and seemingly in the engineering, science and tech industries.

I give these guys a ton of credit for showing up in what might be a fairly gnarly situation. At the end of your time together with each participant, you simply let the facilitators know which one (or ones) you would like to see for a follow-up date, and they introduce you via e-mail soon after. Not a bad idea - at all.

The other benefit of meeting in a public place with other singles is that you have more people to choose from, and it's amazing what you can learn from someone in a social situation. It's incredibly important to notice how people interact and treat others.

So often, it's the little things that matter. What are the person's table manners like, how do they treat the wait staff or others in the group? One of the most appealing qualities is to see and be with someone who treats others with respect and kindness. It's a big turn-on.

Likewise, if someone is impolite, rude and crass - it's a major turn-off. This is equally true in non-dating situations as well. We are all attracted to people who treat others, as they would like to be treated.

No one likes to be with someone who puts down, belittles or simply treats someone else as "less than." It's a major red flag, that doesn't belong in your flag holder. Stay away.

An aquarium is also a great place for a first date. Kids love it of course, but many adults still enjoy watching the underwater creatures. The lighting is comfortable and the colors are wonderful to see.

Some people have asked about going to a movie or baseball game. Again, ask your date what they enjoy doing.

Dating Success After 40

NEIL: The only way I'd take a woman to a ball game or a movie or ballet, is if I know she loves doing those things. But, I'd never do this as a first date because I don't know if there is going to be chemistry or not. If there's no chemistry, then we are both stuck together for two hours. That's no fun for anyone!

I also want to be someplace we can talk and learn about each other. One of my first dates was at a driving range, since we both loved playing golf. She needed to prepare for an upcoming golf tournament, needed some tips on her swing, and I was a low-handicap golfer willing to help her. That was a fun day!

If you're the imaginative type, you might think up something unique and memorable, not the typical date of a movie and dinner—Boring!

You might like some of these ideas:

- Go on a picnic, find a place to rent a boat or a kayak, go for a run together, volunteer a couple hours at a local soup kitchen, or take a cooking class together.
- Check the local listings for events in town, such as a live band, a walking tour of the city, an arts and craft fair, a tour of the botanical gardens, a cornfield maze or a local festival.
- Visit a local brewery, a comedy club or go shopping at the Farmers' Market.
- Racing Go-Karts or going for a horseback ride is plenty of fun, inexpensive and quick. Flying kites together at a park or at the beach is always fun and certainly different for most people. Miniature golf gives you an opportunity to get to know each other, have a few laughs and compete for an hour or so.

NEIL: I had my best first date ever on a sunny day in Boston. We met in a town just a few miles from the city. We liked each other at first sight, so we decided to drive the fifteen minutes to Boston, and then walked along the Charles River for an hour. The chemistry was so fantastic that we went to lunch, which ended up lasting for two hours!

That all went so well that we decided to walk around the North End, which is a great Italian neighborhood with dozens of restaurants. We visited two more restaurants, laughed, ate, enjoyed each other's stories and when we finally shared a good night kiss, realized we'd been together for twelve hours. Now that's a great first date!

I texted her when I got home, told her how much fun I'd had, and asked her to text or call when she was home safely. She texted me as soon as she got home, and we both agreed to a second date.

When the chemistry is there, you know it, you feel it and it seems like you've known each other for years. That's the type of date we hope you enjoy! It may not happen on your first date. But, sooner or later, you find someone with that chemistry that adds a spark to your day!

During your time together, ask your date questions about their interests, hobbies, favorite vacation locations, interesting experiences they've recently had, where they grew up, which college they went to and anything else that ties into the conversation you are having. But don't overdo it: don't ask too many questions, or it will seem like an interrogation.

NEIL: You'll have a sense of the chemistry fairly quickly and probably within the first few minutes. We've done hundreds of hours of research for this book, and the most common complaint from the women is that guys just talk about themselves or their favorite sports teams. It's boring and leads to what we call "a waste of their time!" Take a sincere interest in their life and interests, and you will most likely have a very good first date, if the chemistry is there.

Guys, you need to know that women love to be listened to when they're talking about their feelings, what they enjoy and something meaningful. So pay attention, nod your head, make eye contact, ask them questions to confirm you understand—and share your thoughts. If you do that, you'll be ahead of 80 % of your competition. You can thank me by buying another copy of this book for your six best friends!

And, for my male friends out there, here is one more thing to keep in mind. It's a helpful hint that Nancy has asked me to share with you: Please don't stare at your date's breasts, or worse yet, stare at other women while you're with her. It's the height of rudeness, and no one wants to feel like the person you're sitting across would rather be with someone else. Not a smart move. Period.

NANCY: Both genders like to be heard. So ladies, we need to listen up as well.

Having said all this, we want your first date to be a major success. We also realize this doesn't always happen - especially the first time out.

Either way, major success or not, it's a great experience of getting to meet someone and learn more about yourself in the process. Remember, if at first you don't succeed, try and try again. You'll find yourself on a roll if you keep it up, and you can and will find someone else that catches your eye and shares common interests.

NEIL: Anyhow, there are thousands of others to choose from.

NANCY: Hundreds, if you're a woman seeking a man.

As you already know, we are firm believers in going after what you want in life and not settling for anything less. Nobody is perfectly matched to us, but some are very close! We have those factors in our mind that are "acceptable" and those that are "red flags" and unacceptable. Life is just too short to be with someone you don't enjoy!

Many people on the dating sites are recently divorced, have had horrible sex or none at all for the last twelve years, or were under-appreciated and are now ready to begin a new chapter. Take it slowly. This is a brand new adventure. The first date may lead to a second and many more. By the fifth date, you'll have a better idea of who this person really is.

Warning: A few of our trusted and brilliant female friends have asked us to add this warning: When you're meeting someone for the first time, let a friend know where you are meeting your date. Ask your friend to text or call you thirty minutes after your meeting starts. This serves two purposes. If the date is horrible already, you have an excuse to leave (kids are sick, dog is hungry, need to get a root canal) but it's also a way to let your friend know that you are safe and all is well.

Kimberly Seltzer, of Elite Image Makeovers, offers the following advice for dates:

Have Fun—It sounds so simple, but you need to let

go of the urgency to find that perfect partner. The problem is that neediness and a sense of desperation can cause your potential dates to run for the hills. Instead, make dating fun. Find your inner child again by being playful and light. Avoid interrogating on your first date. Don't ask a hundred questions to see if s/he meets your criteria for marriage. Avoid heavy conversations, talks about politics or religion or bland Q&A sessions that don't create connection.

The key is to be in the moment, authentic and come from a place of curiosity. Avoid prefabricated "lines" which come across as stiff and insincere. Instead, laugh, share stories, keep it light and ignite passion. You'll have plenty of time to get to know them and see if they are the right one.

Kimberly went on to discuss the importance of balance in your dating life:

Compartmentalize Your Life To Create Balance

Many people over 40 describe dating as feeling like they have a split-personality disorder. It can be daunting to bounce from leading a meeting as CEO of your company to playing with your child (if you are a single parent), to meeting someone new for a date. Instead of letting those roles blend together, take the time to separate each one. For instance, if you are at work try to put most of your energy into your professional goals. Think about your date afterwards.

Also, make sure you have allotted some time to shake off that work mode. If you have a date right after work, allow some transition time to relax. Listen to music, talk to friends and change your outfit. Much like a costume change in a play, switching outfits is important

Nancy Michaels & Neil Wood

to help you switch roles. Avoid running from one event to another without some down time in between.

At the end of the day, confidence is the number one element both men and women find attractive in each other. When you feel confident, you attract love and opportunity in your life no matter what age you are! By keeping these simple tips in mind, you might even find dating interesting and exciting. So, get out there and enjoy!

Dr. Diana Kirschner, author of *Love in 90 Days* and *Find Your Soulmate Online in 6 Simple Steps*, has a different view on frequency of dates and how much is too much, too soon:

It is best to date three guys casually without sex (kissing and canoodling is OK) for several months. This means you will not "flame out" by spending too much time with any one man before you know if he is good for you (and then get your heart broken!). Following this program you will naturally have a good reach and frequency of contact with the guy(s) you are really interested in, because your dance card will be full.

After you meet someone who seems to be The One, continue with your dating program of three for at least two months. During that time there should be regular, consistent contact with The One that gets better over time. As the relationship unfolds, he should be more physically and emotionally available and more committed to you. This includes the following:

- He should grow more attentive and loving.
- He should become more open to sharing his feelings, his space and his social life with friends and family members.

- You should feel able to be yourself with him.
- You should find yourself continually surprised at how he fills your needs to be understood, appreciated, romanced and celebrated for who you are.

After there is a clear coming together with some talk of exclusivity and a future together, you can stop the program of three, have sex (make sure it is safe!) and allow more access to you and more time together.

NANCY and NEIL: Many guys are all in favor of dating several women at a time, as Dr. Kirschner suggests. What a surprise!

NEIL: A friend of mind is currently going on dates with five different women. "Variety is the spice of life," he says. He has slept with two of them, but "waited" until the second date, when they asked if they could um…"get to know each other better."

NANCY: Ahem……

NEIL: Both women are classy, intelligent, successful, beautiful and know what they want in life, so don't think they are sleazy or easy. The chemistry with both is fantastic, which is why they felt completely comfortable making love so quickly.

NANCY: I'm "middle of the road" on this point. It's a balancing act to be dating multiple people - especially when juggling kids, work, a home, etc. Although I'm not a prude by any stretch, I prefer to be monogamous when taking a relationship to the next level and deciding to be sexually intimate with a man. I'd also like the courtesy of knowing that a sexual partner is also being intimate with others - primarily for health reasons.

I haven't always followed this rule; however, it's rare to meet with success in a relationship if you move to the bedroom too quickly. Not every man walks away believing their partner is a "classy, intelligent woman. On the contrary, men seem to lose interest more quickly. Let's face it: men are wired to be hunters and we women might want to let them do their job - hunt away. Double standards also still apply.

NEIL: I'm not convinced that a quick sexual connection and acting on it might lead to a "flameout," as Diane suggests. Relationships end for various reasons. Deciding not to have sex for the first three months with someone you are attracted to, may send a message to the guy that you have some major trust issues, don't like sex or don't like him. That potential relationship could end up with both of you being friends at best, and that's all.

NANCY: My concern about the issue of waiting several weeks, even though there's a mutual attraction, is that they may be attempting to hide something, such as an STD, impotence, erectile dysfunction, etc. An honest conversation about these issues might put a potential relationship at risk, but hiding them and using "time" as the excuse for delaying intimacy is not honest either, and the latter two issues mentioned above will be clear when clothes are off and the "time" is finally right. Again, the bigger issue of putting someone else's health at risk is a much bigger concern.

Dating Success After 40

NEIL and NANCY: We do both agree that chemistry in and out of bed is very important to the connection in a relationship. Granted, the first couple of times in bed may not be spectacular, because it takes time to learn what turns each other on, what positions are best for orgasms and the personal intimate boundaries.

First intimate experiences with someone new are like first dates — intensified: you don't know each other well, you haven't learned how to please each other yet, and the result sometimes falls short of expectations. Ladies —and men too —should not judge too quickly, as a partner who is interested in continuing a relationship is usually eager to please and willing to learn.

But waiting for three months? Neil says no, thank you! Nancy's not sure she could wait it out either.

NANCY: A friend of mine was dating a guy she really liked, but he said he was old fashioned and didn't believe in sex until he'd really gotten to know the woman. Four months later, she found out he was basically impotent, and this was something of a serious nature, nothing that could be "fixed." This was a deal breaker for her. She was much younger (15+ years his junior) and sex wasn't as important to him anymore. But to her, well, she just wasn't willing to give that part of life up yet.

Summing up: It's important to see here that different people often have different dating standards. There is no right answer, but each partner in the relationship should have their needs met to satisfy their own values, desires and comfort level at whatever time it happens. We do think it strange if, from the start a man states that he doesn't want sex too soon. It may be a major red flag — especially coming from a man. He may be hiding something more. The point is to find out what your personal balance is, listen to the experts, then decide what is best for you.

Chapter 10

Avoid Bad Counsel - Debunking Dating Advice

We all know "that" person - who loves to offer "sound" and thoughtful dating advice. These folks have the best of intentions, but in reality, many of them are just like the child-LESS individuals who love to dole out parenting advice to, ah . . . parents.

Quite frankly, they're not qualified for the job of giving reputable advice on a topic they know little or nothing about. Most of these suppliers of dating advice have either never been married, or have been married a long, long time and like it that way. They have "theories" about men and women that they love to share, when in reality they haven't had much experience themselves or bothered to gain much knowledge about the subject. Yet, they pursue the conversation knowing little about what it's like to be dating, post-40, in the 21st century. God bless 'em - just don't listen too intently.

NANCY: Some of the bad advice we've heard sounds like something my mom would have said when I was a teenager. Like, "I was a virgin when I married your father (at age 19, I might add), and you should save yourself for marriage, too." I knew, at 16, that this would not be a reasonable option, as I had no plans for marriage in the near future.

Please understand, we having nothing against anyone who wants to "save themselves" for marriage, however, we're not that kind of guy or girl, the second time around.

We understand that men are men and women are women. Even in our 21st century world, the standards, or "rules" for "appropriate dating behavior" for men and women still seem unique to each gender, due to our respective roles in life, within our family, and in society. It seems that's the way we're wired.

We do recognize that times have changed - but we believe the pendulum has swung in the opposite direction in many ways. We now have pseudo-relationship "experts" - friends and family - offering all kinds of bad advice and "strategies" to land a partner.

Some doozies we've heard (particularly from women to other women) are featured in this list of Top 10 Bad Advice Items:

1. Never offer to make dinner for your date (you're not his wife and he should take you out).
2. Don't answer his calls.
3. Don't reply to his text messages right away.
4. Wait three days to follow-up.
5. Never pay for anything - ever.
6. Play hard to get - men are "hunters."
7. Wear suggestive clothing - men love that!

8. Flirt with other men when you're out with him - it makes them crazy! Side note: Crazy all right!
9. Make him take you out for dinner on the first date.
10. Don't give him compliments - keep him wondering if you like him.

NANCY: You get the gist. Now, here's our take on why this is **BAD** advice. Listen up, Ladies - here are my reasons, accompanied by Neil's commentary at a few points, on why you should NOT follow this ridiculous advice:

1. *"Never offer to make dinner for your date (you're not his wife and he should take you out to dinner if he wants to eat)."*

OK, I understand not wanting to replace the role of a wife for someone too early in the relationship. That's having your thinking cap on, Ladies, and I can appreciate that. However, I think making a meal with, or for, someone, in the privacy of your own home; can be a very romantic and intimate thing to do.

It also shows a level of kindness, and hopefully a talent that might end up remaining completely hidden if you never do this. The mere gesture of preparing food is endearing, and even if you're no Martha Stewart or Giada De Laurentiis (I wish!), it won't matter, as long as you made the effort. Honestly, I'm a huge fan of Googling "Easy Fall Entrees" or - fill in your own blank - when it comes to cooking. Why kill yourself over intensely challenging recipes when you don't have to? Some of them are killer delicious, too. Hmm . . . gives us another idea, so stay tuned for our next book - *Recipes to Love By* - just kidding - not happening. I'm an equal opportunity "receiver" and would love and encourage even a hint that a guy wants to make a meal for me. In fact, my one and only husband (so far - and so far, so good), invited me to his apartment around our fifth date for a chicken, rice and broccoli dinner. Was it gourmet? Not so much. Thoughtful and considerate - and therefore, ah . . . attractive? Oh yeah, baby. So, it works both ways. .

2. *"Don't answer his calls."*

Are we pre-pubescent here? If you can't pick up a call because you're on a tight deadline for work, your child broke her arm two seconds ago and you're rushing to the ER, or you're in an important meeting (personally or professionally), we understand. If you <u>can</u> take the call, however, pick up the damn phone!

This is not a Candy Land/Poker game here, Ladies. One sure way of putting a man off is by ignoring his attempts to connect with you. Even if you're not interested in him, manners go a long way in gracefully stopping a relationship from moving further. As one Match.com date of mine told me, "I have feelings too." Touché. Avoidance is passive-aggressive behavior that no one finds "attractive" coming from the opposite (or same) sex. Don't do it. Stop it! Stop it! Stop it!

3. *"Never call him."*

Bam! You'll show him, won't you? How? By being elusive, unavailable and tough to reach. Yeah, nothing turns a man on more than knowing you're not interested. Really? Wrong answer!

Personally, I like to be called first, in the beginning of a relationship. Can't help it - I do. It's the traditionalist in me coming out, I realize. However, after having a few dates and I feel that things are moving progressively forward, I have no problem picking up the phone and asking him out for a date. It could be a dinner party I'm hosting, a local theatre production I have tickets for, or a new restaurant I'd like to try out.

Don't overthink the request to see someone you care about again. I'll bet (Neil, are you listening?) that if you have a gut sense things are going along at a nice pace, the guy would be thrilled that you took the initiative to reach out to him and ask for a date. Now, that's romantic - not desperate.

4. *"Don't reply to his text messages right away."*

Again, this is game playing,.. and it's not the kind of game I like to play with a man (if you know what I mean). Texting is tricky because some of us love it and some of us hate it - particularly those post-60. We get it. We agree, texting - like e-mailing - can be misinterpreted and is certainly not the best way to communicate if there's any possibility of a misunderstanding.

Having said that, if someone texts you and you can text or call back - then do so. We're all adults here, so we should act as such.

5. *"Wait three days to follow-up."*

Men are told to do this, as well. STUPID! Thankfully, Neil has a softer side to him and has already confessed (in Chapter 9) that he'll call the night of a date to see if his date arrived home safely, and also to tell her (if relevant) what a great time he had. Nice guy. We love that about Neil, don't we Ladies?

This 3-day rule is bogus. I will say that I like the man to respond first after a first date, via call, text or e-mail. Call is best, though, as much more can be "sensed" in a voice than in an e-mail or text, don't you agree? After that, game on! It makes no sense to make someone "wait" for some random reason before you let them know you had a good time and/or want to make sure they got home safely. Neil - are you sure you're no longer available? This simply contributes to the prolonging of a follow-up date, if so desired.

NEIL: I agree with Nancy. There are more than five hundred women that fit my search criteria within twenty-five miles of my home. If I call a woman after a date and don't hear back that day, then I'm assuming she has no interest and lacks the manners to say "No, thank you" to a second date. So, I'll just find someone else within my "matches" to ask out on a date. I do prefer a phone call instead of a text, because I can tell so much by the tone in someone's voice.

NANCY: Remember, as we both have pointed out, men act more quickly in the dating process, and ladies - we need to keep up if we're interested.

NEIL: We sure do act more quickly, and some people say we act with a sense of urgency. We only have another thirty or forty years of energy for exciting dating, so there's no reason to procrastinate. *Carpe diem*!
Therefore, we're not fans of this dating "tactic."

6. *"Never pay for anything - ever."*
NANCY: OK, now this is flipping ridiculous.
I appreciate a gentleman picking up the check on the first date. It's chivalrous, thoughtful and . . . appropriate (my opinion). Having said that, I'm ready, willing and able to return the favor and contribute, as well.
Whether that means picking up the movie tickets along with popcorn and water, or the admission fee to the Arboretum, it's all good! Like it or not ladies, most of us are working women and can take care of ourselves.
Here's another reality check - or some other sad/bad news, depending on your outlook. Many of the gentlemen we'll be dating, post-40, have "been there, done that" in terms of financially taking care of a wife and family (and may still have those obligations, as well - as they should). Taking all of that financial responsibility on again, so soon, may be overwhelming.
Please understand, under NO circumstances do we recommend you, as a woman, should "take care" of a man,

Dating Success After 40

financially (Disclaimer: We mention this because women are more vulnerable than men, it seems, to giving complete strangers their life savings in the name of L-O-V-E). Never, ever, ever.

We've seen it happen too many times and it never ends well.

On the other hand, taking a man out, on occasion, or offering to pay for a part of the date, or for something you know he'd like to do, is incredibly thoughtful and sends a message of strength, caring and independence. Personally, I think nothing turns a man on more than a financially independent woman. Call me crazy! Neil . . .?

NEIL: I'm all in favor when a woman offers to pick up the tab or cover the tip, but never on the first date. I'm old-fashioned like that and will always pay for the first, and quite often the second and third date. Many of my female friends have told me stories about how the guy they met for coffee, on a first date, wouldn't even pay for the coffee. Note to Guys: If you can't afford two cups of coffee, don't waste anyone's time, because there won't be a second date. Ladies, I also have a word of caution for you, based on my own experiences and stories from others. If you offer to go on dates just to get free meals, have some respect. One woman told me she had 56 dates in one year, with different guys at her favorite restaurant, and never paid for one! That's a rare breed of woman, thank goodness!

7. *"Play hard to get - men are 'hunters.'"*
The games just keep coming, don't they?
NANCY; We understand that men have a "hunting" gene and women have a "gathering" or "nesting" gene. Men and women have primal instincts and some more "traditional" roles in our society, but again, times they are a changing.'

If allowing a man to follow-up with you, post first-date, is allowing them to be hunters, I say, hunt away!

Personally, I would not play the game of avoiding, or not calling or responding to his repeated messages with the aim of making a "hunter" out of him. If you do this, I will guarantee you he will leave you for road kill and go on to "hunt" another. No more games or deadly sporting activities - puhlease!

NEIL: Nancy is absolutely correct here. There are thousands of beautiful women online within a forty-minute drive, and I love to hunt. Rejection doesn't bother me a bit. I've been in sales for thirty years, so I can take a "No," which is what I believe a woman is saying when she doesn't return my phone call or text. And, I'll only call or text once before I continue hunting, elsewhere.

8. *"Wear suggestive clothing - men love that!"*

NANCY: OK, men may love that in the bedroom when, and if, it gets to that juncture in the relationship, but - my guess is - not so much in public. There is a lot to be said for leaving some things to the imagination. Gender-specific body parts are some of them.

By wearing suggestive clothing, you up the ante on embarrassing yourself (first and foremost), and your date as well. If others are telling you to "get a room" based on your wardrobe, maybe it's time to go home and change—or better yet, look in the mirror before heading out on the town. Whatever turns you on when you're alone, between two consenting adults, we're all for. But until the relationship turns private/intimate, Ladies, please do keep those dainty items in the lingerie drawer at home.

Dating Success After 40

NEIL: Good point Nancy! A woman who flashes the "girls" or wears a skin-tight skirt, just to get the attention of other men while we're on a date, does not impress me. I want to be with a woman who has class. Of course, I know some guys that would prefer the suggestive clothing, since they're focused on one thing only. Second dates don't matter to them, because they are just counting the minutes it takes to get to bed. To each his own, but that's not my mission.

9. "Flirt with other men when you're out with him - it makes them crazy!"

NANCY: Yes, it will make him crazy, alright! Crazy enough to cause a sudden end to the date and, perhaps, never see you again. If this is what you'd like to see happen, this is one way to achieve your goal - but not a nice one.

If the man has any sense of self-esteem and worth, the relationship will end on Date #1. No one appreciates a companion ogling another person (as attractive as that person may be) when the attention should be focused on you. Not a good call - ever! The truth is, there are many people we could find attractive, however, when we're in the company of a new (or old) companion, keep the focus there - not on the hotties that may be around you! Again, mind your manners, people!

10. "Make him take you out for dinner on the first date."

NANCY: As you know, we like a coffee connection the first time we meet. It can be short and sweet if we're not "feelin' the love" or move on to a walk on the beach and, perhaps, a lunch. You don't want to end up like I did once; tying up an entire evening with someone sharing a pizza and drinking club soda with someone you're not feeling it for. Life is short. Move through the initial date(s) quickly.

NEIL: I know several people who did go to dinner or a baseball game on the first date. Within twenty minutes, they wished they'd met for coffee, instead. It's a terrific first date and a perfect quickie to see if you have any chemistry. Save your strength - you'll need it.

11. *"Don't give him compliments - keep him wondering if you like him."*

NANCY: We believe, if you like something or someone, you should say it. Everyone likes and appreciates a compliment, so if you're sincere in liking what someone is wearing, the color of their eyes, their sense of humor - whatever it is - just say it. Both genders like to be complimented.

I once dated someone (a rocket scientist - no joke, true story) and I complimented him on the shade of his sage green sofa. Being left-brained as he was (still is), he wore green shirts on the following few dates. When I subsequently commented on his "love of green," he said he was wearing it because I'd mentioned liking the sage sofa he had. Cute, right? OK, putting "left brains" aside, people like to be told something nice about themselves.

Now, some people (even rocket scientists) like to take compliments to the extreme; nevertheless, it's better to give them than to hold back!

NEIL: I always find something to compliment someone about. I believe it shows a level of kindness and appreciation. As long as the compliment is sincere, it goes a long way and adds to their self-confidence.

NANCY: Much of this Top 10 "bad" advice is not ill-intended but, nonetheless, should be avoided like the plague. At best, it's dated advice and misleading, and at worst could turn off a potential mate in short order.

NEIL: My father had a saying when people offered advice:

Dating Success After 40

"Always consider the source." So, in the dating world that so many of us are engaged in, if a miserable, lonely pessimist gives you any of the wrong advice listed in this chapter, just smile and walk away. We speak from experience and are glad to share our successes with you.

Now, for some really good, 21st century advice; here are some thoughtful, in-depth comments from **Rosalind Sedacca, CCT** on what's really important when it comes to creating a healthy relationship:

Dangerous Don'ts and All-Important Do's — For Healthy Relationship Success

Sadly, disastrous divorces all too frequently make the headlines. Their stories reflect unconscious, unstable behavior, especially when it comes to relationship mistakes.

Far too often, we find shallow singles with star-lit eyes that spend more time working out their wedding details than on determining whether this was a good match from the start. Too many couples think no further than the honeymoon plans when contemplating marriage. They have no idea about the complexity behind real relationship issues and the maturity it takes to create a successful long-term outcome.

Most people learn through hindsight about the challenges two people face when living together week after week, month after month in today's stress-filled world. It takes awareness, flexibility, great communication skills and the ability to understand your partner's perspective to make a relationship work - and that's just for routine life experiences. Throw in accidents, sickness, job loss and other major stressors, not to mention the complexities that come with having children, and it's easy to understand why so many relationships fail and so many marriages end in divorce.

If you're single and looking to find a healthier, happier relationship ahead, or marrying for the first time and want to avoid relationship disasters, here are some tips that are worth serious consideration:

- Know your partner well — during the good times and the bad. It's after you face disagreements, nursing your partner through an illness and other life challenges that you find out who you are really contemplating spending the rest of your life with. If what you discover makes you uncomfortable, have some serious conversations - or move on before making any further commitments.

- Don't expect to be "completed," "saved," or "fixed." No one can fill the void in your inner self. You're setting your partner up for failure if you expect them to fix your problems and love you through your unresolved issues. Do the inner work on yourself first, perhaps with the support of a therapist or coach. Heal your wounds and neediness. Then seek out another soul who has done the same to partner with you.

- Be your authentic self - and don't change for a partner's approval. You can't fake your way through a relationship or a marriage. If you hate sports, the Internet or pets, state it up front and find a mate who loves you knowing this reality. It's unfair to hide your true self from your partner and it's a disservice to yourself pretending to be who you are not. It's wise

Dating Success After 40

to honor who you are. Then look for a partner with high self-esteem who loves himself or herself as they are. That's a formula for lasting relationship success!

As too many singles discover, money won't buy you a happy marriage. You can't use sensuality as a substitute for good sense. Relationships don't have storybook endings. They require constant attention, the ability to sacrifice and compromise at times, and a heavy dose of respect for the person you brought into your life.

Before setting out once again in the relationship world, work on your inner demons, let go of the baggage from previous relationships, and take your time in getting to know the special partner you are choosing. There's no magic wand that will make your relationship succeed, but these guidelines will set you on a course that will circumvent a lot of pot holes along the road to happily ever after.

Chapter 11

Between the Sheets

Recently, we sat down and had a heart-to-heart in order to figure out what's actually going on with couples in the bedroom. During our discussion, it became evident that the majority of advice we receive—from friends of the same gender—may be off base. They are likely not the best resource on how to satisfy the opposite sex - quite the contrary!

We actually learned quite a lot from this sharing of knowledge from the women's and men's perspective, and we're going to share some of that dialogue with you right now:

NEIL: Most of my closest friends are women, and because they feel comfortable telling me anything, and often everything, I usually get an earful when they talk about guys and sex.

NANCY: No kidding, Neil! It's great to have a guy to talk sex with - who better to tell us what turns them on?

NEIL; I agree, Nancy. Guys, listen up, because the comments I've heard from some women are not very flattering. Apparently, most guys still look at sex as a sprint to the finish line and try to imitate the action of a jackhammer.

NANCY: OMG - What a visual - but sadly, so true. They've watched porn movies and think they know exactly what women want. Wrong! OK, I can speak from experience when I say emphatically that most of us women do NOT want to be on top of a desk, with heels on, while someone forces themselves into our bodies from behind. It's just not that fun. Do we agree, ladies? Do NOT believe what you see in porn "films." Please, don't.

NEIL: Some of us men do know better, and view making love as a wonderful, gradual stroll through a beautiful garden, hand in hand with a sexy woman. A confident and experienced guy's goal is to provide his lover with as many orgasms as she can handle over the next hour or evening.

NANCY: Can we give a toast to this man? Really!

NEIL: The guys in the know (the ones who know better) enjoy foreplay, providing delicious and wonderful oral sex, taking time as she gradually builds to a crescendo, providing dozens of soft, sweet kisses all over her body and bringing her to the most amazing orgasms known to women!

Guys, there are 8,000 nerve endings within the clitoral head alone! Now you know why they call the clitoris the "love button." The head of the penis only has 4,000! The biggest mistake many guys make is not paying attention, or being aware of, the sensitivity of the clitoral head. Men, prepare for a feast, and oh, please, take your time! Tease, play, lick gently, explore and you will soon hear fireworks!

NANCY: Whoa, Neil, do you know anyone like this - besides yourself, of course? Inquiring minds want to know. Sadly, there aren't many guys who know how to make love like this.

Why not? I'll bet cavemen might have done better. If not, they might have been hit over the head by the cave woman they were trying to woo.

NEIL: Many women who married when they were very young have never had an orgasm during intercourse. This isn't the women's fault. Maybe their guy just doesn't know how to get them to that point, due to his lack of experience or interest.

Then again, every woman is different. What works for one woman may not work as well for another. Ride 'Em Cowgirl by Dr. Sadie Alison, is a fabulous book for "Sex Positions for Better Bucking."

Many of the 40-something married women I've spoken with still haven't had the joy of an orgasm during intercourse! Keep in mind that only 30% of women can have an orgasm from penetration. The rest of them need the outside stimulation to achieve orgasm. Hopefully, they've at least enjoyed the Big O with the help of a vibrator, or with a guy who is a master with his tongue - maybe both, simultaneously!

According to **Robyn Vogel**, a Boston-based sex therapist: Some women have waves of energy during intercourse or other sexual activity, but they don't identify those waves of sensation as an 'orgasm.' Vaginal orgasms are simply contractions of the vaginal wall - and depending on internal sensitivity - women can be having what are scientifically known as orgasms. Many women do not have orgasms during intercourse; they just aren't as sensitive to internal stimulation as compared to external, or clitoral.

One woman was talking candidly with her 80 year-old mother and her mother admitted that she never had an orgasm during intercourse. Yes, it's a bummer, but the good news is that both men and women can push the "Restart" button and begin anew.

NANCY: OK, I can't help myself - this is pitiful and I cannot begin to accept a reason for such a thing. Ladies, we also need to take some control over our bodies and the pleasure we're able to receive here. Come on! There is nothing wrong - and everything right - with "exploring" our intimate parts and knowing what pleases us so we can articulate this to our partners.

So if you don't know how to reach a climax on your own, I'd encourage you to start trying. There are plenty of "tools" out there - nice ones, not hammers or screwdrivers - that can help you along the way. You'll see some examples towards the end of this chapter.

In addition, if you ask any woman who has experienced fantastic lovemaking, they'll tell you it's worth it! Buckle up, because you are about to experience Nirvana!

Neil, we women want to know, when will your international speaking tour of Teaching Men How to Please Their Partner be starting? Sign us up!

NEIL: Well, Nancy, as you know, in marketing, we do extensive Market Research to discover exactly what customers want and what will satisfy them to the point at which they become "raving fans."

Robyn Vogel:
When we open ourselves up to dating again, after the trauma of divorce, we may feel insecure about our ability

Dating Success After 40

to flirt, approach someone we are attracted to, or initiate a connection. If it's been years since we've been in the dating scene, well - we may be behind the times! Almost everyone is online now. Ease your way into this new experience. It gets easier with time and practice.

NEIL: I asked many of my female friends what women want, what they feel is missing during sex, and to describe their best lovers. They were all very open with me, and I learned a great deal very quickly (this was "Pre-Nancy" - as I'm sure you would have been happy to share your views, as well). The summation was that guys don't get it when it comes to pleasing a woman.

I do want to defend my "brothers," though, and can corroborate the fact that guys don't get much "how to wow a woman training" as teens or young men.

But- so what? We're all adults now, and as some-one recently shared with Nancy - "no one loves a selfish lover." Agreed. In business, we need to take responsibility for our success. We should do this as lovers and partners in our personal relationships as well.

Ya think?

The assumption is that men are supposed to know how to be a sexual master, so they fumble around and believe they are doing well if they have a good explosion. If guys focus on what turns their lover on and provide it gently, slowly and with presence, then holy hallelujah, it's going to sound like Heaven just opened the pearly gates and the horns are screaming with excitement and joy!

NANCY: Amen, Neil!

NEIL: In a recent group study at The Sunset Bay Spa

and Resort, every woman agreed that when their lovers totally satisfy them and provide them with one, or several, orgasms to make them smile and sigh, they will gladly reciprocate. We call that a Win-Win in sales, marketing and life.

This study group also noted that women in their 40s and 50s going through peri-menopause or menopause are happy if they feel aroused, never mind having "enough orgasms," implying multiple.

So guys, ask what they like and what arouses them. Again, "nobody loves a selfish lover." Period. Giving and receiving is the name of the game here, guys.

Sales professionals refer to this as the Law of Reciprocity, which states that all transmissions of energy result in a return of energy, in like kind. It's a cousin to the Golden Rule, which states, "do unto others as you would like others to do unto you."

OK, so now that we have your attention and perhaps your excitement meter is rising, the question on the minds of most is how to begin. There are thousands of instructional DVDs that show how to perform various treats with your lover. There are also movies on the instructional online sex websites, so don't just turn to porn sites as your role model. The ways they have sex is not realistic. It's too aggressive and lacks sincere passion and tenderness.

NANCY: Really, Neil? Give us the list of the legitimate, helpful sites- so we can share it with our man!

NEIL: The Sinclair Institute and its Better Sex info is one of the best online resources for sex toys, "how-to" videos and sex education information. You can even view their videos on YouTube, if you like. Of course, you can watch and learn alone, in the privacy of your own home and or, even better, with your lover. Get ready for some playtime!

NANCY: Two heads are always better than one - in my experience. The same is true for intimacy and sex.

NEIL: As you watch these instructional movies, you'll see just how much women like being treated gently, with kindness, tenderness, love and affection. This certainly isn't Screwing 101.

NANCY: OK, part of me just wants to say "Duh?" Are you guys seriously thinking that women don't want this kind of lovemaking? Really? This is all about making love. Thank you, Neil - glad to know someone is "getting it."

NEIL: Maybe you have never experienced anything like this in your past, so keep this in mind - the past does not determine the future. Begin again.

NANCY: And maybe, just maybe, when looking at past relationships, it's some of the reason the two of you "before" are not here in the "now" and future. It's a shame, baby - a cryin' shame. But, as Neil states, it's never too late to begin again.

NEIL: In marketing, we often use the term "new and improved" after a product has gone through a slight or major overhaul. You can do the same quite easily, IF you are willing to try. The rewards are tremendous and worth every lesson!

NANCY: Can I just say, "Praise the Lord!" - or whatever higher powers you believe in?! Thank you, sweet Jesus - is what I'd say! Finally, a grown man who "gets" it, ladies. Neil is a keeper! Spread the word, my friends - spread the word!

NEIL: These videos and movies are very useful to singles and couples alike, who are open and willing to learn. We are marketing and sales gurus, so we always enjoy reading and doing research! I've read two dozen books on how to be a great lover, what women want in bed, the art of oral sex and how to arouse a woman to have multiple orgasms every time you are together.

NANCY: Whoa, whoa, whoa! I have to be honest with you . . . ah, ah . . . men. I, and I'm sure other women, have experienced men who are very focused on wanting to be pleased - orally and otherwise, with NO mention of how they might want to do the same. Wrong answer, ladies and gentlemen. What are they thinking? We all want to love and be loved. Please - listen to Neil.

NEIL: Yes guys, every time! I learned things I wished I'd known when I was 25, because my sex life would have been totally different. However, it's never too late and I know enough now to make my girlfriend beam with joy, every time.

NANCY: Let's toast to that! A gentleman I recently met said that when he was in the military and stationed in Japan at age 18, he visited a more "mature" lady of the evening. She was in her mid-thirties, and after their first meeting she suggested he return so she could teach him the art of making love to a woman.

He was intrigued and returned later that week. She gave him the lesson of a lifetime. He's still grateful to this woman, who simply taught him how to be an exceptional lover, and how to satisfy a woman, first. Life changing for him - and I'm sure others - who benefited from this woman's gift of the lesson on lovemaking.

Look at this as a fun exploration with your lover or on your own. Go beyond your current comfort zone.

As a client of mine recently phrased it, "What's your ask?" You have to be willing to lay it on the line and simply ask for what you want. If I'm willing to ask, I would expect and want you to do the same. Come on Ladies and Gentlemen - we will achieve more intimacy if we simply ask, show and tell our partner what we're looking for.

NEIL: Another important thing to realize, guys, is that while performance in bed is important, many women are looking for sincere intimacy and emotional fulfillment. They are done with lazy lovers and want a deeper, more meaningful relationship. If you can provide all of this and be wonderful and attentive in bed, you may discover some of the happiest moments and days of your life.

Marketing and advertisers entice you to try new products by telling you what the product will do for you. We love that concept! We can tell you that with enhanced skills and greater confidence, you will experience more pleasure than you've ever enjoyed - if you're only willing to try!

Robyn Vogel:
The most loving thing you can do for your partner is ask them how they want to be loved, and then give it to them.

NANCY: Good advice, right, Neil?

NEIL: Yes! Try new things, but also know where your boundaries are. We believe that whatever two consenting adults agree to do with one another is A-OK. We get that some things may take practice (and lots of it), but practice is fun and the rewards are . . . as MasterCard says - priceless.

If you don't feel comfortable with some of the things you try in the bedroom, talk about it openly and honestly. Not everything is for everybody. No big deal. We recommend that you never allow yourself to be forced into something you don't want to do. Never, ever, ever.

It's much easier to try new things when you feel comfortable and safe with your lover. As trust builds over time, you or your partner may be willing to try more variety in bed. Take your time, be leisurely and keep it playful. Too many guys treat lovemaking like a quickie.

NANCY: OK, I know that I'm about to contradict myself, but I have to say that although we prefer a lover with a "slow hand" and "easy touch," quickies can be goodies when needed! Just something to keep in mind.

Robyn Vogel:
Deep, intense and amazing orgasms sometimes result after a long, slow and delightful build with plenty of teasing.
NANCY: Boys - we love that! Really and truly!
NEIL: Guys, we want to give you a bonus hint that will pay dividends and add delicious icing to the cake while you both lie there smiling. The best companies on the planet focus on high-level customer service, after their products are purchased and enjoyed by customers. They follow up to ask how happy and satisfied the customer is.
NANCY: Right on, Neil - that's what we're saying here. A happy customer - or "lover"—is what it's about. Ideally, two people should be and feel this way, so- go for it!
NEIL: Learn from the follow-up example set by quality

customer service, and take a similar approach with your lover. Ladies like to refer to this as "pillow talk" after you've cleaned up and crawled back into bed. Look into your lover's eyes and tell her what you really enjoyed while you were making love. Touch her hair, caress her skin, and make direct eye contact with her.

Ask her what she enjoyed, and be sure you pay attention to what she says. In sales, this is known as Consultative Selling. You ask questions, and then you listen intently to the answer. You then ask another question or two, to confirm that you understand exactly what they mean.

Ande Lyons, host of the popular *Loving & Lasting* radio and online show, offers this advice:

Gents, don't forget snuggling and cuddling is often a woman's favorite dessert! In order to fully express herself sexually, a woman doesn't just bare her body; she pulls back the curtains and shares everything she has - emotionally, spiritually and physically. This view into her soul often leaves a woman feeling vulnerable - and the snuggling and cuddling makes her feel loved, accepted, and appreciated.

It also gives her time to recover and restore, resulting in increased arousal, and leading to more intimate stroking... and, perhaps, another round of sensual pleasure! Finally, the brain LOVES snuggling because it releases one of our favorite hormones, Oxytocin, which is why we feel so close and intimate while snuggling. So, be sure to cuddle and snuggle while you're asking your "follow up" questions.

NANCY: Whoa - OK, we love Neil - and just reading these words - well, does something internally to our mind and body. Bring it on, Gentleman! We're ready, willing and able to experience this type of lovemaking.

NEIL: OK, but as they say in the commercials — wait, there's more: there are toys and books that help the erotica and sensuality of lovemaking that are joys to enjoy. Come along, people…

Ladies and gentlemen, there is a book that should be required reading for all lovers who want to know how to give a woman the most incredible orgasms she's ever had.

Foreplay is very important to warm a woman up to the point at which she can begin to have her first orgasm. Guys, we know it doesn't take you very long before you can explode. Eh, what is it? Four or five minutes are just about enough for the guys? Women need a little more time.

NANCY: OK, Neil - that's true. However, when all is said and done, some women can more easily climax in the way they've requested or "asked" for it - just sayin'. Again, ask your partner what turns him or her on and be willing to fulfill those desires. This is how a true and intimate connection can occur.

Now is a great time to introduce a terrific resource for all of you - have no fear. Go to www.betterafter50.com - it's a great online newsletter. Once you're there, check out an article on the very subject we've been talking about, entitled "Warm Me Up Baby: More Foreplay Equals Better Sex," published in the September 19, 2013 issue.

According to **Walker Thornton**, author of the article, the average male takes 4-5 minutes to reach orgasm, maybe longer when adjusting for age. For a woman it can take 20 minutes or more. We are not built for quickies! So, when a guy rushes in, gives you a quick kiss or two, gropes a breast and proceeds with intercourse, chances are she's still dry — not aroused and possibly frustrated.

Or - pissed off and certainly not in the mood for immediate intimacy - if you're going too fast. We need a little more warming up, particularly if we've had a stressful day or our head's just not in that place. We need transition. We need to feel loved, desired and wanted. We need foreplay.

What is foreplay?

Technically, foreplay is:

A set of intimate psychological and physical acts between two or more people meant to create desire for sexual activity and sexual arousal.

—Princeton University

Yay! That's what we're talking about guys! Bring it on!

Also:

Foreplay is a vehicle for creating or increasing arousal. We need to think more expansively about how we build and sustain arousal. It's a mistake to think that a few minutes of touching and kissing is sufficient for us as women. Arousal involves getting our mind engaged as well as our body. We may not be in the mood, but through foreplay that could change. More of us would be having sex if we, women and men, understood that concept. How long is enough? 10 minutes? An hour? How about foreplay as something that exists between couples throughout the day? A state of mind paired with specific actions designed to elicit response in a partner… or in ourselves — because we share responsibility for creating a sexually receptive mood.

— Walker Thornton

NEIL: Amen, people - this is what we're talking about. Ultimately - we all want to feel desire and want to be desired by someone. There's nothing like an equal balance of love meeting love and connecting on that level. Sharing yourself physically and emotionally with someone is the most intimate and connected you can be with someone. There's no replacement.

Now I want to tell you about the book that will explain how to give your woman mind-blowing orgasms. The title is *She Comes First*, by **Ian Kerner, PhD**. It's known as the thinking man's guide to pleasuring a woman. I can tell you, from personal experience, that this book will provide you with enough info that you'll have a Masters degree in clitoral pleasure.

NANCY: Praise the Lord! I get that men can reach their peak early, but there's no bigger turn-on than when one of the duo can wait for their partner to be satisfied. Here's a huge secret - when that happens - you're in luck too, gentlemen!

NEIL: I bought a copy of *She Comes First* three years ago when I "suddenly" became single after 24 years of marriage. My mission was to find out how to treat a woman to the best orgasms she's ever enjoyed. You should see my copy of it! I've taken more notes and dog-eared more pages than I have in any college book I ever owned.

NANCY: Neil, we want a copy of your dog-eared book - so we can clone it and give it to our partners! Give us the pages that were most important to you - or us. Don't hold back!

NEIL: Well, Nancy, in the book it teaches you how to arouse, tease and savor a woman during foreplay.

NANCY: Yay, that's what we're talking about! I am speaking for all women here!

NEIL: *Cosmopolitan* magazine praised it as "Every man's must-read." Tell your guy to put down the remote and pick up She Comes First.

The back cover states:

According to sex therapist Ian Kerner, oral sex isn't just foreplay, it is coreplay: simply the best way to lead a woman through the entire process of arousal time and time again. She Comes First is a virtual encyclopedia of female pleasure, detailing dozens of tried-and-true techniques for consistently satisfying a woman and ensuring that sexual fulfillment is mutual.

Well then, did I make my point? Do your woman a favor and order one today! I guarantee that if you follow the steps, practice, and ask your woman for guidance while you treat her and take your time, you will both experience more joy than you can imagine! Have fun!

NANCY: OK, this dialogue has just brought back a rather unpleasant moment in my sex life, when I was on the receiving end of a conversation that focused on what I could do for him - get it? I'm not a prude and am happy to please my partner. But again - it's not all about one person - especially the man. Why? Because, as Neil so eloquently put it, the time it takes for one person (a female) to climax versus another (a male) is a matter of 15 minutes or more. Patience, my friend(s), patience!

NEIL: Many people who divorce after having married at a young and inexperienced age have not experienced a very good, creative and orgasmic sex life. Sadly, they don't know what they are missing. But wait, it's never too late to explore.

Besides consulting websites, videos and books, you can learn about all the great toys in the marketplace that can help stimulate women to enhance their pleasure and orgasms.

The Magic Wand, for example, can be purchased on Amazon or Drugstore.com for about $65.00. I recommend the electric version, which is listed as a massager. Oh it'll massage her, alright! Turn up the music, so you don't frighten the neighbors!

Robyn Vogel:

Betty Dodson (Author, PhD and Leading Global Sex-

ologist) **and Good Vibrations** (stores and website) are good resources, too. Be careful, though - using vibrators is a wonderful way to experience pleasure but it also can contribute to decreased sensitivity.

NANCY: Any other toys you can recommend, Neil?

NEIL: While you're shopping, you might as well get a few more treats. Look at the Rabbit, the Bullet, the 7 Speed Bullet, Love Egg and the Orb. Two of the best vibrators are the LELO Ina 2 and the JimmyJane Form 2. They should come with a warning however, because the orgasms will blow your mind and most likely cause the neighbors to call 911... Just sayin'.

NANCY: Wow, I've heard of some of these and think they're probably awesome ... Do go on, Neil. I'm willing to learn more. How is this, that a man knows more about sex toys than we (I) do?

NEIL: Take a chance, and browse around the store with your lover. If you don't find enough toys on Amazon. com, then look at www.MySecretLuxury.com. You'll find some websites that offer better prices for some of these great vibrators and toys, but they may be toxic. Enough said on that point. We want you to have fun and stay healthy. The best lubricant on the market is the all-natural Aloe Cadabra. It's 95% organic aloe and wonderful to use.

NANCY: Oh, Neil, the things we wished we knew 15 years ago. But better later than never!

NEIL: Folks, if you are over 40 and finally willing (and able) to enjoy some great sex, go for it! If you feel like spicing up your new sex life a bit more, then check out and enjoy the Tantra Sex Chair at www.tantrachair.com. This is a game changer my friends! Be safe of course. We believe some of the BEST sex you've ever experienced is right around the corner. Be creative and have fun!

Chapter 12

It's a Wrap!

As Neil Sedaka once sang, "They say that breaking up is hard to do. . ." and we can safely say - this is true.

The challenges of finding yourself suddenly single at mid-life are not for the faint of heart. Add to it, venturing out on the dating scene, post-40, can be outright daunting. Many of us have been out of practice in the fine art of getting to know potential partners. We experienced what you may be confronting now and faced the task at hand of re-tooling ourselves before "getting out there" again. That's why we wrote Dating Success After 40.

There is, though, a silver lining that we fully believe to be true. There are many people - far more than one - that we could be compatible with. So much of the "compatibility quotient" has to do with geographic proximity (or willingness to travel), timing, mutual interests, where and how we meet others, and being open to finding love again. — and yes, some miscellaneous, random and stroke-of-luck chance encounters.

As marketing and sales professionals, however, we believe your chances are increased 10-fold if you apply business development principles to finding love. If Coca-Cola stopped advertising, Pepsi would gain market share.

If you're not out marketing yourself and networking in areas (online and offline) where you're most likely to meet other single people - you're not marketing yourself to be part of a couple. Assuming that's your goal (since you've bought and are reading this book), you're doing yourself and others a disservice.

We hope that *Dating Success After 40* will be of help to you as you navigate your own path to finding true love and a relationship that complements you and your desires to be coupled. There are many great things about growing older and acquiring so many personal attributes along the way - including perspective, maturity, knowing oneself more intimately, clarity of expectations in a relationship, and so much more.

It was our intention to share with you our experiences and those of others, along with the advice of proven experts on various dating-related topics—all focused on providing you with the keys to dating success after 40.

Most of us know a wonderful happy ending to a match gone right, as well as ones that have gone not-so well. This book was written, designed and created to clue you in on this amazing journey. It is our sincere wish for you that you can find love - again, or for the first time, and that it be everlastingly wonderful.

Nancy just came back from an Ireland wedding where two people who knew each other most of their lives (one grew up in Ireland and the other summered there and still lives in the United States) got married in their mid-fifties for the first time - to one another. If that doesn't give us all hope, we're not sure what does. Long-distance love aside, the bride and groom and all of their guests at this true "destination" wedding couldn't be happier! Their song, "At last, my love has come along. . ."

We hope the same will be true for you! Take a chance to find that true love. Share your success stories with us and we will share your happiness. Wishing you success, enriched happiness and years of smiles!

Meet the Experts

Stacey Alcorn

Entrepreneur, Author, Business Owner, Attorney, Blogger and Mom. Stacey Alcorn's keynotes, blogs, and radio show continue to offer a compelling message about defining and achieving your dreams. Her message is one of building upon everyday small successes as a catalyst to reaching greater accomplishments. To bolster triumphs even further, she shares a message of tuning out naysayers, focusing on constructive energy, and every individual's fundamental ability to mentor others to greatness. Stacey blogs regularly on her own site and writes for The Huffington Post. She also hosts The Road Map to Wealth Radio show across the country on WBZ once a month on Saturday nights. Stacey has become a highly sought after keynote speaker and consultant because her concepts about building a phenomenal business are extracted from her own experience in launching, building, and operating four successful businesses, which she continues to operate today.

She also mentors and consults start-up firms and Fortune Global 500 businesses.
http://www.StaceyAlcorn.com

Anthony Ambrose
Known for his adventurous cuisine, Chef Anthony Ambrose brings the wealth of experience and specialty techniques to his eclectic menus. Chef Ambrose began his culinary career in New Jersey, where he received accolades from The New York Times. In 1987, Tony was recruited by The Hotel Meridien to become the first American chef de cuisine for its premiere dining room, Julien. Tony worked with two-star Michelin chef Olivier Roellinger in France and Boston and in 1993 Ambrose opened his first independent restaurant venture, Ambrosia on Huntington. Ambrosia was soon named one of the top 25 new restaurants in the country by Esquire magazine, the best new restaurant in Boston by the Boston Magazine annual reader's poll, one of Boston's best restaurants by Bon Appetit, and one of the most popular new restaurants by the 2000 Zagat Boston Restaurant survey. He has appeared on the Food TV Network, Live with Regis and Kathy Lee, and Celebrity Chef's Cook-Off. He was also invited as a guest chef for the James Beard Foundation Great Regional Chefs of America Series.
http://ambrosiaeventsandcatering.com/thechef.html

Ginger Burr

For 27 years, Ginger Burr, President of Total Image Consultants, has helped women around the world create a wardrobe they love by connecting with their inner essence. Ginger directs corporate seminars and community education programs for some  of Boston's most prestigious organizations including Harvard Law School, Harvard Business School, the U.S. Army, and Fidelity Investments and has been the media spokesperson and fashion expert for Rowenta, Inc. A notable speaker and leader in the field of fashion and style, Ginger's adroit understanding of beauty trends and fashion image has been celebrated by The Boston Globe, Women's Health Magazine, Worth Magazine, Forbes Magazine, Bloomberg Business Week, Elegant Wedding Magazine, cnn.com, ABCNews.com, Fox TV News and More Magazine.com. She is the author of That's So You! http://totalimageconsultants.com

Cija Black

Cija Black is a dating and relationship expert, author, speaker and educator. Her dating and relationship expertise comes from 20 years of in-the-trenches experience safely using personals and online dating sites. She is the author of Modern  Love: The Grownup's Guide to Relationships & Online Dating and creator of the online Udemy class: Sorting

Your Love Baggage. Cija is dedicated to helping people sort their relationship baggage, take responsibility for their happiness and find real love. To find out more visit: http://www.modernloveguide.com

Dr. Diana Kirschner

Dr. Diana Kirschner appeared on Oprah and starred in a PBS TV Special on love. She is a clinical psychologist who has helped thousands all over the world to create greater self-esteem and more loving relationships. Dr. Diana's website, Love in 90 Days is a leading source of dating and relationship advice. She is the author of Find Your Soulmate Online in Six Simple Steps and the best-seller, Love in 90 days.
http://www.Lovein90Days.com

Ande Lyons

Ande Lyons is the founder and Chief Passion Curator for Bring Back Desire, where she tastefully and playfully shares tips, tools and resources with women who want more sensuality and sexual excitement in their lives. As the host of the Loving and Lasting Radio show, Ande helps couples stay tuned in and turned on to each other through her engaging and informative conversations with love experts, relationship experts, and authors.

Ande's eBook; Loving and Lasting: How to Stay Tuned in and Turned On in Marriage has been a best seller in the marriage category on Amazon.com. Twenty of Ande's favorite Love Experts share their best advice on how to have a more meaningful and fulfilling marriage. An enthusiastic and experienced entrepreneur with an MBA and several successful businesses to her credit, Ande is enjoying a well-balanced life (really!) managing her growing business while raising two wonderful boys with her husband.

Loving and Lasting Radio Show: http://www.blogtalkra-dio.com/andelyons

http://www.bringbackdesire.com/about-bring-back-de-sire/ (Naughty)

http://andelyons.com Loving and Lasting (Nice)

Susan Ortolano

Susan Ortolano, M.A., PCC, CMRC is an Intuitive Relationship Coach and Educator who combines her skills as a trained Relationship Coach with her gifts as a Clairvoyant and Intuitive. She has guided many singles to shift their old paradigm and  prepare for and find the great love of their life, along with many couples that are partnered and panicked. With her unique guidance, clients take their committed relationships in new and more loving directions. Susan has had her own story, having experienced infidelity and decep-

tion in her own marriage and the resulting divorce, to finding the great love of her life. She is happily married to her husband Rick, also a Counselor and Coach, is a proud Auntie and Godmother, and works with clients all over the world from her home in Southern California.
http://www.conciossoulmates.com
http://www.radiantpathways.com

Rosalind Sedacca

Rosalind Sedacca, CCT, is a Divorce and Relationship Coach and founder of the Child-Centered Divorce Network for parents. She is also the co-author of 99 Things Women Wish They Knew Before Dating After 40, 50 & Yes, 60! and True Love At Last for Women Over 40: Answers You Need for the Relationship You Want! Rosalind is a Contributing Writer for WE Magazine for Women, an Expert Blogger for The Huffington Post, an Advisor at ParentalWisdom.com as well as a Contributing Writer for KidzEdge Magazine, Exceptional People Magazine and Cupid's Pulse. She's the 2008 First Place Winner of the Victorious Woman Award. Rosalind's books, courses and programs for single women can be found at:
http://www.womendatingrescue.com and her free eBook on Smart Dating Advice for Women Over 40: Answers to Your Most-Asked Questions are available at http://www.womendatingafter40.com.

Kimberly Seltzer

Kimberly Seltzer is an image expert, dating coach and matchmaker. She draws upon her experience as a therapist and helps clients all over the world to unveil their most beautiful self. Whether it's updating your image or transforming your dating life, her philosophy is simple. Work from the inside out to achieve your goals and boost your self-confidence. She holds a LCSW and after practicing as a therapist for over 10 years, she moved to California and trained with one of the top Image Consultants in Los Angeles, Ashley Rothschild, at The Rothchild Image. She obtained a certification in Style Coaching through the Style Coaching Institute in the UK which teaches the unique combined use of life coaching, NLP and styling. Most recently, she ran the VIP division at one of the largest nationwide matchmaking companies, Elite Matchmaking in Beverly Hills, CA where she infused image consulting and dating coaching as part of this unique matchmaking process. She has been featured in Cosmopolitan Magazine, Fox News Magazine, Yahoo!Shine and The Examiner. http://www.eliteimagemakeovers.com

Robert Siciliano

Robert Siciliano, CEO of IDTheftSecurity, is fiercely committed to informing, educating, and empowering Americans so they can be protected from violence and crime in

the physical and virtual worlds. His "tell it like it is" style is sought after by major media outlets, executives in the C-Suite of leading corporations, meeting planners, and community leaders to get the straight talk they need to stay safe in a world in which physical and virtual crime is commonplace. Siciliano is accessible, real, professional, and ready to weigh in and comment at a moment's notice on breaking news.

http://www.IDTheftSecurity.com

Emmi Sorokin

Emmi started performing makeovers for people in 1990 and she launched, It's a Man's World Image Consulting out of her passion for making men stand out from the crowd for all the right reasons. Today, Emmi is the only woman in the Boston area who specializes exclusively in men's image makeovers. "A man's wardrobe is his most immediate tool for success, how he dresses impacts everything from how much money he can make, to how much admiration and respect he receives. "My clients get more action in the boardroom and the bedroom." Emmi received her degree in fashion design from Burdett College and mastered personalized customer service over a decade of managing clothing stores. Her experience allows her to negotiate better prices and service on behalf of her clients. Her guiding principles are simple: Have him look better than ever and save him time and money.

http://businesscasualsurvivalguide.com

Jodi R. R. Smith

Jodi R. R. Smith began promoting better behaviors in 1986 and founded Mannersmith Etiquette Consulting in January 1996. She continues to serve as president. Her extensive background in motivational psychology and human resources has reaffirmed her belief that proper manners and etiquette are an essential part of functioning successfully in today's world. Jodi has been seen on the NBC Today Show, Good Morning America and on the CBS Early Show. She has been quoted in the Washington Post, Wall Street Journal, New York Times and USA Today. She has been a featured guest on radio shows from coast to coast and into Canada. Jodi holds a bachelor's degree in motivational psychology from the University of Rochester and a master's degree from Cornell University. She is also the author of three etiquette books. From Clueless to Class Act: Manners for the Modern Man and From Clueless to Class Act: Manners for the Modern Woman and The Etiquette Book: A complete Guide to Modern Manners
http://www.mannersmith.com

Rosanne J. Thomas

Rosanne J. Thomas, founder and president of Protocol Advisors, Inc., believes that "Professional Presence" is attainable by everyone. A Certified Business Etiquette and International Protocol Consultant, Ms. Thomas began dispensing business etiquette advice more than 20 years ago at Tiffany & Co. where she was employed as a Corporate Account Executive. After eleven years at Tiffany & Co. as top sales producer, Ms. Thomas gained professional Business Etiquette and International Protocol certification in 1995 and founded Protocol Advisors, Inc. Today, Ms. Thomas combines her wealth of experience with continuing cutting-edge research, offering learning programs that address the real issues professionals face every day. From first impression management to social media savvy, Ms. Thomas covers all aspects of "Professional Presence" in a highly entertaining, experiential and results-oriented way. Her charm, humor, grace and expertise create enjoyable learning experiences that inspire pride, drive excellence and impact the bottom line. The results: unsurpassed personal, professional and financial achievement.

http://www.protocoladvisors.com

Robyn Vogel

Robyn Vogel is a Couple's Intimacy Therapist and Sex Coach, Certified Sex Educator, mother, entrepreneur, and all around love-adventurer! She is dedicated to guiding couples towards the most deeply loving connection possible; which very much includes great sex! Robyn brings joy, wisdom, humor, warmth and powerful, accessible tools to support others in their own healing. Robyn has been a regular featured contributor for Self Growth, Your Tango and Woman's Tool

Box. Look for her in the March 2014 issue of Redbook Magazine! TV appearances include Sex for Her Health and Happiness! Workshops include: An Introduction to Tantra, The Energetics of Intimacy, Sex After Kids, Shy About Tantra, The Dance of Intimacy, Communication as Foreplay, and her weekend workshop, Awaken the Fire Within. Robyn is a Licensed Mental Health Counselor (LMHC) in the state of Massachusetts.
http://sacredtantricfire.com

Susan Winter

As seen on Oprah, best-selling author/relationship expert Susan Winter ("Allowing Magnificence" and "Older Women/Younger Men") specializes in today's evolving forms of loving partnership. Her credits include: The Today Show, Good Morning America, ABC/CBS/NBC Evening News, VH1, and CNN. Feature articles and cover stories include: Cosmopolitan, Harpers Bazaar, People, Good Housekeeping, New York Times, Washington Post, London Times, Boston Herald, Las Angeles Times, Chicago Tribune, San Francisco Chronicle, In Touch Magazine, Entertainment Weekly, Woman's World and The Time of India. In radio Susan has been a frequent guest on NPR, ABC, Playboy Network (Sirius Radio), CBS News Radio and 98FM-Dublin, Ireland.
http://www.susanwinter.net

About the Authors

Neil Wood is the President and CEO of Neil Wood Consulting. He's one of the most popular keynote speakers in North America and has given more than 5,000 presentations through-out his career. His company focuses on teaching people how to market themselves and their business by  communicating their value more effectively. His marketing background and expertise have helped thousands of people provide a clearer message to those they are trying to reach, attract, inspire and captivate.

Neil became an expert in online dating after getting divorced. He found online dating to be a perfect way to meet women who had the specific characteristics he was looking for. Online dating worked so well that he wanted to coach others on how to find a match and, perhaps, the love of their life. There are more than forty million people involved in online dating sites, and that number is growing rapidly every year. Neil has begun a series of online dating success seminars in the Boston, Massachu-setts's area and is planning a nation-wide expansion. His mission is to help more people create profiles that attract their perfect match for love and romance.

To learn more about Neil please visit http://www.neilwoodconsulting.com.

 **Nancy Michaels** has developed consulting and coaching programs to create unique marketing and sales propositions for satisfied clients such as Office Depot, Walmart, UPS, Xerox, Wells Fargo, HP and many others. As CEO of her business, Grow Your Business Network, she created a process to attract and retain valuable customers, focusing on brand loyalty and the generation of new clientele to ignite quick results.

During the past 20 years Nancy has consulted, spoken and taught in 42 states to more than 60,000 entrepreneurs and has been featured in numerous media outlets. She hosted OfficeDepot.com's Web Café Series of on-line seminars for more than a decade. Previously, she was publicist for Matt Lauer, current co-host of the Today show.

Nancy is the author of six books including, Stripped! 49 Life Lessons Learned from Dying, which chronicles her own personal story of love, marriage, separation, illness, and divorce. Nancy's philosophy is that business is about relationships and she used that principle to reinvent herself, both professionally and personally, leading to her ultimate triumph through incredible challenges.

Nancy's strength, resiliency and sound business background put a face on the world of adult midlife dating. She created websites on how to navigate the post-40 dating world, penned an article for More.com, and produced online videos and hosted webinars - attracting callers from around the world.

To learn more about Nancy please visit www.nancy-michaels.com.

Made in the USA
Lexington, KY
16 February 2014